Salomon Lane

Voice of Eternity
The Apocalypse of Apostle Peter

Original Title: Voice of Eternity
Copyright © 2025, published by Luiz Antonio dos Santos ME.

This book explores the vision of the Apostle Peter regarding the Apocalypse, unveiling profound interpretations on spiritual themes, final judgment, salvation, and hope in challenging times. Through captivating narratives and detailed reflections, the work invites readers on a journey of introspection and faith.

1st Edition
Production Team:
Author: Salomon Lane
Editor: Luiz Santos
Proofreader: Ambrósio Nunes
Cover: Studios Booklas / Amadeu Rossi

Publication and Identification:
Voice of Eternity / By Salomon Lane
Booklas Publishing, 2025
Categories: Religion / Biblical Studies / Apocalypse
DDC: 236.9 - CDU: 27-3

All rights reserved by:
Booklas Publishing / Luiz Antonio dos Santos ME

No part of this book may be reproduced, stored in a retrieval system, or transmitted by any means—electronic, mechanical, photocopying, recording, or otherwise—without the prior and express authorization of the copyright holder.

Summary

Salomon Lane 6
Prologue 9
Chapter 1 The Call 12
Chapter 2 The Judgment 15
Chapter 3 Paradise 18
Chapter 4 Hell 22
Chapter 5 The Fallen Angels 26
Chapter 6 The Giants 29
Chapter 7 The Flood 32
Chapter 8 The Tower of Babel 36
Chapter 9 Sodom and Gomorrah 39
Chapter 10 The Exodus 43
Chapter 11 Mosaic Law 47
Chapter 12 The Prophets 51
Chapter 13 The Messiah 55
Chapter 14 The Cross 58
Chapter 15 The Tree of Life 61
Chapter 16 The River of Life 64
Chapter 17 The Gates of Paradise 67
Chapter 18 The Eternal Fire 71
Chapter 19 The Outer Darkness 74
Chapter 20 The Demons 77
Chapter 21 The Antichrist 80

Chapter 22 The Beast of the Apocalypse 83
Chapter 23 The Number of the Beast 86
Chapter 24 The Great Tribulation 89
Chapter 25 The Rapture 93
Chapter 26 The Second Coming 96
Chapter 27 The Millennium 99
Chapter 28 The Final Judgment 103
Chapter 29 The Date of the Apocalypse 107
Chapter 30 Humanity's Destiny 110
Chapter 31 Salvation 113
Chapter 32 Free Will 116
Chapter 33 Original Sin 119
Chapter 34 Divine Grace 123
Chapter 35 The Resurrection of the Dead 126
Chapter 36 Heaven and Hell 129
Chapter 37 Life After Death 132
Chapter 38 Reincarnation 135
Chapter 39 Purgatory 138
Chapter 40 Limbo 142
Chapter 41 Predestination 145
Chapter 42 The Apocalypse in Popular Culture 148
Chapter 43 The Meaning of the Apocalypse 152
Chapter 44 Hope in Difficult Times 155
Chapter 45 The Importance of Faith 158
Chapter 46 Love for Others 161
Chapter 47 The Pursuit of Justice 164
Chapter 48 Forgiveness and Reconciliation 167

Chapter 49 Life in Community 170
Chapter 50 Caring for Creation 174
Chapter 51 The Pursuit of Peace 177
Chapter 52 The Value of Human Life 180
Chapter 53 Individual Responsibility 183
Chapter 54 The Legacy of the Apocalypse of Peter 186
Epilogue 192

Salomon Lane

Salomon Lane is a professor of theology at the University of Bradford, where he is dedicated to teaching and researching the origins of Christianity and its developments throughout history. With an academic and methodological approach, he is recognized for his ability to contextualize Christianity within the complex social, political, and cultural structures of the periods in which it evolved.

Born into a family that valued education and historical knowledge, Lane showed an early interest in history and religious texts. His academic background includes studies in theology, ancient history, and comparative religious studies. He completed his undergraduate studies and focused his research on Christian apocryphal manuscripts and their influences on contemporary theological thought.

Throughout his academic career, Lane has devoted himself to exploring ancient manuscripts and documents, both in European archives and international collections. He has visited several historically significant museums, such as the British Museum and the Vatican Library, and has gained access to manuscripts crucial for understanding early Christianity. Among these are the Nag Hammadi Manuscripts, discovered in Egypt in 1945, and the Qumran manuscripts, also known as the Dead Sea Scrolls. These primary sources have allowed Lane to deepen his analysis of non-canonical Christian texts and to better understand the theological and cultural contexts in which these texts were produced.

In addition to his dedication to teaching and research, Lane actively participates in international seminars, conferences, and academic debates. He is frequently invited to discuss topics such as the relationship between apocryphal texts and canonical gospels, the role of heresies in shaping Christian dogma, and the connections between Christianity and other contemporary religious traditions. His studies are widely cited in academic papers and theses related to early Christianity.

Among Salomon Lane's most significant contributions are his investigations into the impact of apocryphal texts on modern understanding of Christianity. He is the author of numerous articles published in specialized journals, as well as academic works addressing themes related to early Christianity and apocryphal scriptures. His approach emphasizes the importance of understanding these texts not only as historical documents but also as significant expressions of theological and philosophical debates of their time.

One of Lane's main areas of interest is the interpretation of the Gospel of Judas, one of the texts found in Nag Hammadi. He explores how this gospel provides an alternative perspective to the traditional narrative about Judas Iscariot, suggesting a different role for him in the story of Jesus. Lane argues that such texts should not be seen as threats to Christian tradition but as opportunities to broaden the understanding of the diversity of early Christian thought.

Another central aspect of Lane's work is the analysis of cultural and philosophical influences on early Christianity, including contributions from Greco-Roman thought and Hellenistic Judaism. His research examines how the philosophical ideas of the time shaped the development of Christianity and influenced the formulation of its central dogmas and doctrines.

In his books, now available through Booklas Publishing, Lane presents his studies in detail, grounding his analyses in primary sources and academic commentaries. He strives to provide readers with a profound and comprehensive understanding of issues surrounding early Christianity, while maintaining academic rigor. His works are aimed at both academics and readers interested in deepening their knowledge of the subject.

The book that follows is one of Salomon Lane's contributions to the field of Christian history and apocryphal scriptures. The work reflects his commitment to detailed research and his passion for uncovering the mysteries of the past, always with a critical and investigative perspective. Through his writings, Lane seeks to foster a greater understanding of the origins and developments of Christianity, contributing to academic dialogue and the cultural and spiritual enrichment of his readers.

Prologue

For centuries, humanity has accepted the Apocalypse attributed to John as truth. However, many assert that John was not one of Christ's twelve apostles, as commonly believed, but rather a disciple. In fact, the Apocalypse of John was written between 81 and 96 AD. Considering studies that suggest Jesus was born between 4 and 6 BC, John's Apocalypse would have been written 50 to 62 years after His death. Now, before us emerges a forgotten revelation: the Apocalypse of Peter. Written by the apostle who walked alongside Jesus, witnessed His miracles, and heard His most intimate words, this gospel offers an unparalleled vision of the ultimate destiny of creation.

This extraordinary manuscript, discovered in 1886 in Akhmim, Egypt, is more than a mere historical record. It bears the weight of spiritual truth from a man chosen by Christ to be the cornerstone of His Church. Preserved through the centuries, perhaps hidden due to its depth and its challenge to traditional interpretations, Peter's text resurfaces to illuminate minds and reignite souls.

Peter's vision is intense and unwavering. He does not describe the end of times as a series of distant or allegorical events but as a vivid testimony, marked by the conviction of one who saw with his own eyes the fate of the righteous and the wicked. His words are clear: divine judgment is real, inevitable, and imbued with justice, but also with mercy for those who choose the path of light.

The discovery of this text was a landmark event. Found in an Egyptian tomb alongside other fragments dating back to the early Christian era, it reached us in a fragile state but complete in its message. The authenticity of the document and its content shook scholars and believers alike, offering a glimpse into an apostolic vision rarely explored. Peter, whose voice resonates with the authority of one who stood beside the Master, describes not only the horrors of the final judgment but also the glory reserved for those who persevere.

Unlike John's Apocalypse, filled with symbolic imagery and open interpretations, Peter presents a direct and deeply human account. He not only saw but felt the magnitude of judgment and salvation. His words are not merely a record of future events but an urgent plea for all to understand the gravity of what is to come. He speaks of the victory of the saints, the torment of the wicked, and the redemption reserved for those who walk in righteousness.

Throughout the pages you are about to read, you will encounter an apocalyptic vision that resonates with the authority of an apostle, a man whose faith was forged in the fire of proximity to Jesus. Peter guides us through a world where the heavens open, where angels descend to fulfill the divine plan, and where Christ Himself is both judge and redeemer.

This text profoundly impacted those who first read it. By the late 19th century, scholars and theologians were confronted with truths that transcended common interpretations. It was as though Peter's voice, silenced for so long, could finally be heard, and his message resonated in a modern world still striving to comprehend eternal purpose.

Peter's words are a call to reflection and action. He does not present a story to be coldly analyzed but a truth to be lived. His vision of the Apocalypse is not merely a future event but a spiritual reality already in motion, inviting each of us to take a stand. Are you prepared to hear the voice of an apostle? Are you ready to face the revelations that transformed those who dared to read them with an open heart?

This is not an invitation but a declaration: the Apocalypse of Peter is not just another ancient text. It is a voice that transcends centuries, demanding attention, challenging our complacency, and guiding us toward eternity. The time is near, and the destiny of humanity is inscribed in every line of this gospel. As you turn these pages, you are not merely reading a book; you are encountering a truth that could change everything.

    Luiz Santos
    Editor

Chapter 1
The Call

Peter awoke abruptly, his breath catching as if his spirit had been pulled back from the edge of an infinite void. The air in the small room seemed alive, heavy with an unseen presence that defied comprehension. In that moment, silence reigned, but it was a silence that held weight, as though the world itself waited for the first utterance of a revelation.

The fisherman-turned-disciple sat still on the earthen floor of his modest dwelling, bathed in the faint, otherworldly glow of dawn filtering through the wooden shutters. Yet the light seemed unlike the familiar radiance of the sun—it felt imbued with something divine, a reflection of the vision that had seized him.

The vision had not been a dream. It was more real than anything Peter had ever known, more vivid than the shimmer of the Sea of Galilee under the midday sun. In it, the heavens themselves had split open, revealing a scroll etched with fiery words, unreadable yet fully understood. Across that scroll, destinies were inscribed: the fate of nations, the fall of stars, the judgment of all creation.

A voice had spoken, resonant and vast, filling the heavens and his soul. "Peter, son of Jonah," it said, "rise and see what is to come."

In his vision, Peter stood upon a precipice overlooking the whole of existence. Before him stretched realms unimaginable—some gleaming with the light of the eternal, others shadowed by anguish and fire. The voice spoke again, guiding him through this celestial panorama.

"Behold the righteous," it said.

Peter turned and saw a multitude ascending into a boundless light, their faces serene and radiant. They sang with voices that blended in perfect harmony, a melody that spoke of peace, love, and joy unending.

But the vision shifted, plunging him into a chasm of darkness. Flames licked at the edges of the abyss, and a cacophony of cries filled the air. These were not the cries of simple pain but of souls burdened with eternal regret.

"And this," the voice continued, "is the destiny of the wicked.".

Peter recoiled, his spirit aching under the weight of the vision. It was not mere fire or torment that consumed these souls but the unbearable realization of separation from the divine.

Peter's mind raced as the vision drew him deeper. He saw humanity laid bare, their lives illuminated by a light that revealed every hidden deed and thought. The choices of each soul wove their destiny, a tapestry of actions, beliefs, and repentance—or the lack thereof.

A great and luminous gateway appeared before him, shimmering with the radiance of eternity. Beyond it lay a realm of indescribable beauty, where rivers of living water flowed through meadows of light, and the air itself carried the essence of love.

"This," the voice said, "is the inheritance of those who walk in righteousness."

Then Peter was cast down again, this time to a pit filled with shadows and anguish. Here, a different gate stood—massive and ironbound, creaking under its own weight. Through it poured the anguished cries of countless souls, a lament that rose and fell like waves of a dark sea.

"And this," the voice said, its tone heavy with sorrow, "is the inheritance of the unrepentant."

The vision ended as abruptly as it began, leaving Peter gasping for breath. His spirit felt both burdened and alive, as though touched by the very hand of God. He staggered to his feet, his surroundings seeming almost unreal after the celestial panorama he had just witnessed.

Outside, the world continued as it always had. The Sea of Galilee lay calm, the village stirred to life, and the wind whispered through the olive trees. Yet Peter knew that nothing was the same.

He sought solitude in the hills, returning to places where he had walked with his Master. He prayed fervently, asking for understanding and strength to bear the task he now knew lay before him.

One evening, as the first stars began to pierce the twilight, the voice came again—not in a vision but in the quiet depths of his spirit.

"You are the rock upon which I build," it said. "And now you must speak of what you have seen."

Peter returned to the faithful, his words carrying the weight of the vision. He described the destinies of the righteous and the wicked, urging all to repent and embrace the path of light. His voice trembled with urgency, for the visions were not just revelations but a warning—a plea for humanity to turn away from the darkness.

"The time is near," he declared, his eyes alight with a fire that seemed not of this world. "Repent, for the kingdom of heaven is at hand. Choose now whom you will serve."

As Peter spoke, the crowds responded in myriad ways. Some wept openly, confessing their sins and seeking God's mercy. Others turned away, their hearts too hardened to accept the truth. Yet Peter did not falter, for he knew his role was not to convince but to proclaim.

He would speak until his last breath, bearing witness to the divine revelations entrusted to him. Through his words, the call to repentance and the promise of redemption would echo across the ages, carried by the Spirit that had first called his name.

Chapter 2
The Judgment

The heavens stretched wide before Peter, a vast canvas upon which the destiny of humanity unfolded in terrifying clarity. In the stillness of his vision, he saw the world laid bare—its deeds and misdeeds written indelibly into the eternal fabric of creation. The voice that had guided him returned, its resonance like the toll of a great bell, summoning all to attention.

"Behold," it commanded, "the judgment of the living and the dead."

Peter's spirit trembled at the gravity of those words. He was no stranger to the teachings of judgment; he had heard the Lord himself speak of the day when all nations would be gathered before the throne of God. But to witness it unfold in such stark detail was another matter entirely. The vision offered no room for ambiguity, no veil to soften the harshness of divine truth.

A vast throne, radiant with a light that no eye could fully endure, stood at the heart of the vision. Its brilliance illuminated all creation, exposing every hidden corner of the human heart. From the throne emanated a presence both majestic and terrifying, a presence Peter recognized as the Almighty, whose judgment was perfect and unyielding.

Before the throne, multitudes were gathered—innumerable as the stars, yet each soul distinct and visible. They stood in a great plain, their faces reflecting every emotion: fear, hope, despair, and joy. Among them were the mighty and the meek, the rulers of nations and the nameless masses, brought together in perfect equality under the gaze of the Divine.

Peter's attention was drawn to two books that rested before the throne. One shimmered with golden light, its pages alive with the breath of eternity. The other was darker, bound in iron and emitting a shadowy aura.

"These are the books of life and death," the voice explained. "In them are recorded the deeds of all who have walked upon the earth."

As the books opened, the wind seemed to carry the whispers of countless stories, each one a testament to the choices made by humanity. The righteous were called first, their names inscribed in the Book of Life. Peter watched as they stepped forward, their faces radiant with peace.

They were clothed in garments of pure white, and their hands were lifted in praise. The throne spoke to them—not with words but with a voice that resonated in their very souls. They were welcomed into a kingdom of light, their joy complete, their journey fulfilled.

But then the second book opened, and the air grew heavy with sorrow. From its pages, dark clouds rose, swirling around those whose names were written within. These were the unrepentant, the proud, the cruel, and the deceitful. They were summoned one by one, their deeds brought forth as a testimony against them.

Peter recoiled as he witnessed the anguish etched on their faces. Some wept bitterly, their regret too late to alter their fate. Others stood defiant, their pride intact even in the face of divine judgment.

"To the unrepentant," the voice declared, "belongs the outer darkness, where there is weeping and gnashing of teeth."

A chasm opened before the throne, its depths shrouded in shadow and fire. Into this abyss, the unrepentant were cast, their cries echoing into eternity. The sight pierced Peter's heart, a reminder of the weight of free will and the consequences of a life turned away from God.

Yet amid the solemnity of judgment, there was hope. Peter saw figures emerge from the shadows, souls who had been lost but found their way to redemption through repentance. The mercy of the throne reached even to them, drawing them into the light.

The vision spoke of a justice that was perfect, balanced by a mercy that defied understanding. Each soul was judged according to its deeds, but none was beyond the reach of divine grace.

"The judgment is not for destruction," the voice said, "but for the fulfillment of all things. Each must stand accountable, yet my mercy endures forever."

As Peter emerged from the vision, the weight of what he had seen pressed heavily upon him. The world around him, so seemingly ordinary, now felt charged with eternal significance. Every act, every thought, seemed imbued with meaning, a thread in the grand tapestry of judgment.

He began to speak of the vision to those who would listen, describing the great throne, the books of life and death, and the eternal destinies that awaited humanity.

"Choose wisely," he urged them, his voice filled with both urgency and compassion. "The time is near, and the Lord's judgment is perfect. Seek his mercy while it may still be found."

Some heard his words with trembling hearts, resolving to turn from their sins and embrace the path of righteousness. Others scoffed, dismissing his message as the ravings of a man consumed by visions.

But Peter was undeterred. The truth of what he had seen burned within him, compelling him to proclaim the coming judgment to all who would hear.

Through his testimony, Peter reminded humanity of a truth that echoed across the ages: the choices of this life are not without consequence. They shape the eternal destiny of every soul, inscribing their names in the books of life or death.

And as he spoke, Peter prayed fervently that all who heard his words might choose the path that leads to life, heeding the call to repentance before the day of judgment arrived.

Chapter 3
Paradise

A radiant vision unfolded before Peter, as if a veil had been lifted from the edge of creation, revealing the unimaginable splendor of Paradise. It was not merely a place but a realm of infinite beauty, where the very essence of existence resonated with love, peace, and divine harmony. Peter stood in awe, his spirit overwhelmed by the glory of what he beheld.

The air was alive with melodies, not crafted by human hands but born from the heart of creation itself. Each note was a thread in an eternal song, weaving through the golden light that suffused everything. The atmosphere shimmered as if infused with the breath of God, and every corner of the realm seemed to echo with His presence.

Peter's gaze was drawn to a vast expanse of gardens, where trees of unearthly majesty reached toward the heavens. Their leaves sparkled like jewels, and their fruit glowed with a light that seemed to contain the promise of life eternal. Rivers of crystal-clear water wound through the land, their currents carrying an energy that refreshed the soul more deeply than any earthly spring.

"This is Paradise," the voice said, gentle yet resonant. "The inheritance of the righteous and the dwelling of those who have walked in My ways."

As Peter moved through the gardens, he saw figures clothed in garments of pure light. Their faces shone with a peace that surpassed understanding, their eyes reflecting a joy that knew no end. They walked hand in hand, their steps unhurried, as though time itself had yielded to eternity.

In the distance, a great city arose, its walls adorned with every precious stone and its gates fashioned from single pearls. The city's streets were paved with gold so pure it was transparent, reflecting the light of a glory that had no earthly comparison.

The voice continued to guide Peter, revealing the depths of Paradise. "Here, all tears are wiped away, and death is no more. Neither mourning, nor crying, nor pain shall exist, for the former things have passed away."

Peter's heart swelled at the realization. This was not merely a place of rest; it was the fulfillment of every promise, the culmination of the divine plan for humanity. Here, the righteous were not simply preserved—they were transformed, their souls made complete in the presence of their Creator.

He saw a great multitude gathered before a throne that radiated light and love. They worshiped with voices like rushing waters, their praise ascending like incense to the One who sat upon the throne. Angels surrounded them, their wings shimmering with hues that defied description, joining in the eternal hymn of adoration.

The throne's occupant, though shrouded in glory, was unmistakable to Peter. It was the Almighty, whose presence filled all of Paradise with an infinite warmth that embraced every soul.

Peter was led to a river, its waters more vibrant than any he had seen. The river flowed from the throne of God and the Lamb, winding through the city and nourishing the land. Beside it stood the Tree of Life, its branches heavy with fruit that gave life to all who partook of it. The leaves of the tree, the voice explained, were for the healing of the nations.

He marveled at how everything in Paradise seemed to exist in perfect harmony. There was no strife, no division, only unity under the sovereign love of God. The righteous dwelled together as one family, their joy untainted by jealousy or fear.

Peter felt the weight of his earthly burdens lift, replaced by a sense of peace so profound it brought tears to his eyes. He understood now what his Master had meant when He spoke of the kingdom of heaven. This was the ultimate reward for those who remained faithful, the home prepared for them since the foundation of the world.

Yet even in the midst of such glory, Peter's thoughts turned to those who were not present. The absence of the lost, those who had rejected the call to repentance, cast a shadow upon his joy. He knew that Paradise was open to all, but it required a choice—a willingness to surrender one's will to the will of God.

The voice, sensing his sorrow, spoke again. "Do not grieve for those who have chosen another path. My justice is perfect, and my mercy extends to all who seek it. Paradise is not denied to anyone who desires it with a pure heart."

The words comforted Peter, though the ache in his spirit remained. He resolved anew to proclaim the truth of what he had seen, so that none might be lost due to ignorance or neglect.

The vision began to fade, but its brilliance remained etched in Peter's soul. He was drawn back to his earthly surroundings, where the world seemed dim in comparison to the glory of Paradise. Yet he knew that the light of what he had witnessed could shine even in the darkest corners of humanity's existence.

Peter gathered the faithful and spoke of the heavenly kingdom with a fervor that could not be contained. "I have seen the dwelling place of the righteous," he told them. "It is more beautiful than words can express, a place where God's presence fills every heart with unending joy."

His words inspired hope among his listeners, their spirits lifted by the promise of a better world. Some wept with longing, their hearts yearning for the day when they would walk the golden streets of Paradise. Others resolved to live lives of greater faithfulness, determined to secure their place in the eternal kingdom.

Peter continued to speak of Paradise, his testimony a beacon of hope in a world often shrouded in despair. He knew that the vision was not given to him for his sake alone, but as a gift to all who would hear and believe.

And though his heart ached for those who remained indifferent, Peter's faith in the ultimate triumph of God's plan remained unshaken. For he had seen Paradise, and he knew that its gates were open to all who would choose the path of righteousness.

Chapter 4
Hell

The vision descended like a storm, abrupt and overwhelming, pulling Peter into a place where light itself seemed hesitant to tread. Before him stretched a vast and desolate wasteland, shadowed by an oppressive darkness that moved as if it were alive. The air was heavy, filled with a soundless weight that pressed against his spirit, and the very ground beneath him seemed to writhe in agony.

"This," the voice intoned, solemn and unrelenting, "is the destiny of the wicked."

Peter's breath caught as his eyes adjusted to the dim, flickering light that emanated from rivers of molten fire snaking through the expanse. This was no ordinary fire; it burned not for destruction but for torment, consuming endlessly yet never devouring. The land seemed to groan under the weight of countless souls, each one engulfed in a suffering that words could scarcely convey.

As Peter took a trembling step forward, his surroundings came into sharper focus. The cries of the damned rose like a cacophony, an unending lamentation that echoed across the barren plains. These were not cries for mercy, but the anguished wails of souls fully aware of their choices, consumed by the bitter fruits of their own deeds.

Figures moved within the shadows, their forms distorted by suffering and despair. Some were bound by chains of their own making, forged from pride, greed, and malice. Others wandered aimlessly, their faces twisted with regret, their hands clawing at the air as if seeking an escape that would never come.

Peter recoiled at the sight, his spirit heavy with sorrow. These were not strangers but men and women who had once walked the earth, their lives intertwined with the fate of creation.

"Why must they suffer so?" Peter whispered, his voice breaking.

The answer came not as condemnation, but as truth. "Their suffering is not inflicted by my hand, but by their own. The fire is the reflection of their hearts, the darkness the shadow of their rejection of the light. They have chosen this path."

Among the tormented, Peter saw familiar faces—kings who had ruled with cruelty, merchants who had traded in deceit, and priests who had corrupted the sacred for personal gain. Their cries were not of innocence but of bitterness, lamenting the opportunities they had squandered.

The vision shifted, drawing Peter deeper into the abyss. He came upon a great chasm, its depths obscured by a swirling void. From within, he heard voices, not crying out, but murmuring in seductive tones. These were the tempters, the fallen angels who had led humanity astray, their whispers weaving lies into the hearts of the living.

"Do not be deceived," the voice said. "Their power is great, but it is granted only by the willingness of those who listen. Resist, and they flee. Embrace them, and they bind you."

Peter's heart clenched as he saw the tempters' hold on the souls around him. They offered false comfort, feeding the pride and desires that had led to the damnation of many. Yet even here, Peter sensed a faint glimmer of possibility—a chance for repentance, should a soul turn and seek the light.

The torment of Hell was not uniform. Peter saw lakes of fire where souls writhed in agony, their cries swallowed by the roar of the flames. Others endured a cold so biting it seemed to freeze their very essence, their suffering a mirror of the apathy and cruelty they had shown in life.

One scene stood out: a man burdened by a great weight, struggling to ascend a steep hill. Each time he neared the summit, the weight would drag him back down, and he would begin again.

"This is the punishment for his arrogance," the voice explained. "In life, he placed himself above others, refusing to carry the burdens of his fellow man. Now, he bears the weight of his pride."

Peter wept at the futility of it all. Yet he felt no anger toward these souls, only a deep sorrow for the choices that had led them here.

Amid the despair, Peter noticed something unexpected: the faintest trace of light, distant and weak, yet unmistakable. He turned toward it, drawn by its presence.

"What is this light?" he asked.

"It is my mercy," the voice replied. "Even in Hell, my presence is not wholly absent. For those who truly repent, there is hope. But few seek it, for it requires a humility that eludes them."

Peter was stunned. He had thought Hell to be the final, inescapable destination of the wicked. Yet here, even in the depths of torment, the possibility of redemption remained, albeit a narrow and seldom-trod path.

The vision revealed a single soul, kneeling amid the flames, crying out not in anger or despair, but in genuine contrition. The light grew brighter around this figure, and Peter saw an angel descend, lifting the soul from the darkness.

"Repentance," the voice said, "is the key. Even here, it can open the way to salvation. But the will to repent must come from within."

As the vision began to fade, Peter felt a profound heaviness settle over him. The reality of Hell was not merely a place of torment, but a testament to the consequences of human freedom. It was the culmination of a life lived apart from God, where the light of divine presence was all but extinguished by the choices of the soul.

When he returned to the world of the living, Peter wasted no time. He gathered those who would listen and spoke of what he had seen.

"Hell is real," he said, his voice trembling with the weight of his testimony. "It is not the wrath of God that sends souls there, but the rejection of His love. Yet even in the depths of despair, His mercy can reach you. Repent while there is still time."

Some responded with fear, resolving to change their ways. Others scoffed, dismissing his words as the ravings of a zealot.

But Peter could not remain silent. He knew the truth of what he had seen, and the responsibility of bearing that truth burned within him like an unquenchable fire. He would proclaim the reality of Hell not to frighten, but to awaken—hoping that through his words, even one soul might turn and find the path to salvation.

For in the balance between light and darkness, every choice mattered, and every soul was worth saving.

Chapter 5
The Fallen Angels

Peter's vision deepened, carrying him back to the beginning of time, where the eternal heavens shimmered in pristine harmony. In the celestial realm, before the foundations of the earth were laid, the angels moved in glorious unity, their voices lifting in eternal praise of the Creator. They were beings of light, crafted to serve and reflect the infinite beauty of God's holiness.

But even in that radiant expanse, a shadow had formed.

"Behold the rebellion," the voice intoned, and Peter's spirit trembled as the scene unfolded before him. He saw a mighty angel, more brilliant than the others, standing apart. His form radiated an extraordinary beauty, but his eyes burned with an ambition that marred the perfection of his being.

"This is Lucifer," the voice said, "the morning star, who sought to ascend above his station."

Peter watched as Lucifer, once the chief of the heavenly host, gathered others to his cause. Their rebellion was subtle at first, a whisper of dissatisfaction, a seed of pride planted in fertile ground. These angels, captivated by Lucifer's charisma and beauty, began to question the order established by the Creator.

"We are not mere servants," Lucifer declared, his voice both melodic and venomous. "Why should we bow when we are made of light, resplendent and glorious? Let us ascend above the throne and claim what is ours by right!"

His words resonated with those who were willing to listen, and a great divide formed in the heavens. The unity that had once defined the angelic host was shattered, replaced by discord and rebellion.

The Creator, in His infinite patience, did not act immediately. Instead, He allowed the rebellion to run its course, granting each angel the freedom to choose whom they would serve.

Peter was then shown a moment of unspeakable consequence. The heavens trembled as the rebellious angels, now numbering a third of the host, rose up against the throne of God. Their forms, once radiant, began to twist and darken, reflecting the corruption within their hearts.

At the center of the rebellion stood Lucifer, his pride unyielding, his beauty now a shadow of its former brilliance.

In response, the Creator summoned Michael, the archangel, who stood resolute in his loyalty. With a voice like thunder, Michael cried, "Who is like God?" and led the faithful angels into battle against the forces of darkness.

Peter's spirit quaked as he witnessed the war that ensued—a clash of unimaginable power. The heavens became a battlefield, as swords of light clashed with weapons forged from the darkness of rebellion.

The faithful angels fought with the strength of their devotion, while the fallen wielded their pride and defiance as their weapons. The battle raged across the celestial realms, its echoes reverberating through the fabric of creation.

In the end, the rebellion was crushed. Michael and his host triumphed, and the fallen angels were cast out of heaven. Peter saw them plummet like shooting stars, their descent a fiery cascade that marked their fall from grace.

The voice spoke again, solemn and unyielding. "Lucifer became Satan, the adversary, and his followers became demons, chained to the darkness they chose. Their fate was sealed, but their enmity against the Creator and His creation continues."

Peter was shown the abyss into which the fallen angels were cast—a place of torment and imprisonment, prepared for those who had defied the will of God. Yet he also saw how Satan and his minions roamed the earth, seeking to corrupt humanity and draw souls away from the light.

The vision shifted, and Peter was shown the consequences of the fallen angels' actions on earth. Through deceit and manipulation, they whispered lies into the hearts of men and women, sowing seeds of pride, greed, and hatred. Their influence was insidious, weaving through the fabric of human history and culture, leaving a trail of destruction in its wake.

Yet Peter also saw how their power was limited. They could tempt and deceive, but they could not force a soul to turn from God. The choice remained with humanity, and the light of divine grace was always greater than the darkness of the fallen.

The voice offered Peter a warning: "Do not underestimate their cunning, for they are ancient and wise in their rebellion. Yet fear not, for my Spirit is with those who seek me. Resist the darkness, and it will flee."

Peter returned to the earthly realm with a renewed sense of urgency. He spoke to the faithful of the war in heaven and the ongoing battle for the souls of humanity. His words carried both a warning and a promise.

"The fallen angels seek to devour, but their power is nothing compared to the love of God," he declared. "Do not give them a foothold in your heart. Cling to the light, for it is stronger than any darkness."

His testimony inspired vigilance among his listeners. They prayed for strength and discernment, seeking the protection of the Almighty against the snares of the adversary.

Peter continued to proclaim the truth of the fallen angels, urging all who heard him to remain steadfast in their faith. He reminded them that the battle was not theirs alone but was fought alongside the hosts of heaven, under the banner of the Creator.

And though the memory of the rebellion filled him with sorrow, Peter found hope in the promise of ultimate victory. For he knew that the light would prevail, and the darkness, no matter how fierce, would one day be vanquished forever.

Chapter 6
The Giants

The vision carried Peter into the ancient depths of human history, a time when the earth was young and the boundaries between the heavenly and earthly realms were less defined. He stood on a landscape untouched by the scars of modernity, where the air was thick with the presence of forces both divine and profane.

"This," the voice said, resonant with sorrow and gravity, "is the time of the sons of God who abandoned their station."

Peter's spirit quaked as he saw majestic beings descend from the heavens, their forms radiant yet marked by a strange and growing pride. These were the watchers, the angels charged with observing and guiding humanity. But as they looked upon the daughters of men, their admiration turned to desire, and their duty gave way to rebellion.

"They defiled their purpose," the voice continued. "Lust overtook them, and they took for themselves wives from among humanity."

Peter watched in astonishment as the unions between the watchers and humans bore strange and terrifying offspring. These were the Nephilim, the giants of old, whose presence brought chaos and corruption to the earth. Towering over mortals, their strength was unparalleled, their intellect formidable, and their appetites insatiable.

The Nephilim dominated the lands, bending humanity to their will. Cities rose under their rule, built with feats of engineering beyond human capability. Yet their dominion was not one of peace but of oppression and bloodshed.

"They became a scourge," the voice said. "Their existence was an affront to the order of creation, a mingling of the divine and mortal that brought only destruction."

Peter saw the fear in the eyes of the people, their prayers rising to the heavens as they sought deliverance from the giants who had made themselves gods among men.

The corruption spread like a plague, not only through the actions of the Nephilim but through the knowledge imparted by their fallen fathers. Peter was shown how the watchers taught humanity forbidden arts: the crafting of weapons, the secrets of alchemy, and the manipulation of creation for selfish ends.

These gifts, meant to elevate and enlighten, instead became tools of domination and destruction. The balance of the earth was thrown into disarray, and violence filled the land.

The voice spoke again, its tone heavy with judgment. "The earth groaned under their weight. Their deeds defiled the land, and the cry of the innocent reached my ears."

Peter was then shown a council in the heavens, where the Almighty proclaimed judgment upon the watchers and their offspring.

"They shall not go unpunished," the voice declared. "The watchers shall be bound in chains of darkness until the final judgment, and the Nephilim shall be wiped from the face of the earth."

Peter witnessed the execution of divine justice. Angels of might descended, binding the rebellious watchers and casting them into the abyss. The Nephilim, though powerful, were no match for the wrath of God.

The earth itself became a weapon against them. Torrential rains fell, rivers swelled, and the ground quaked. Entire cities crumbled under the weight of divine retribution, and the mighty giants were swallowed by the flood.

As the vision shifted, Peter saw the aftermath of the judgment. The earth, once overrun by the Nephilim and their wickedness, was cleansed. Humanity, though diminished and humbled, began anew. Yet traces of the Nephilim lingered—

ancient ruins, myths, and the faint memory of giants who once walked the earth.

"These remnants," the voice said, "are warnings to the generations that follow. Let them remember the consequences of rebellion and the justice of the Almighty."

Peter also saw that the spirits of the Nephilim, unable to ascend to the heavens or descend to the abyss, became wandering entities, seeking rest but finding none. They were the unclean spirits, the demons that plagued humanity, a perpetual reminder of the corruption born from the union of heaven and earth.

When Peter returned from the vision, his heart was heavy with the weight of what he had seen. The story of the Nephilim was not just a tale of the past but a cautionary account of the dangers of pride, lust, and the misuse of power.

He shared the vision with the faithful, describing the fall of the watchers, the rise of the giants, and the divine judgment that followed.

"The Nephilim were mighty, but their might was their undoing," Peter warned. "They remind us that no power, no ambition, can stand against the will of God. Let us walk humbly, lest we too be cast down."

Peter's words stirred both awe and fear in his listeners. Some pondered the ancient mysteries, their faith strengthened by the knowledge of God's justice. Others wrestled with the implications, their hearts troubled by the echoes of rebellion that still lingered in the world.

Yet Peter remained steadfast in his mission, knowing that the truth of the Nephilim was a part of the greater revelation entrusted to him. Through their story, humanity was reminded of the boundaries set by the Creator and the consequences of crossing them.

And as Peter continued to proclaim the vision, he prayed that the lessons of the giants would not be forgotten, but would serve as a beacon of wisdom for generations to come.

Chapter 7
The Flood

The vision swept Peter into the primordial world, where the earth was young and humanity's numbers had begun to grow. The land was fertile, the rivers abundant, and the skies vast and unbroken. Yet beneath this outward beauty, a deep corruption festered.

Peter stood in the midst of a teeming city, its streets filled with the sights and sounds of a people consumed by their own desires. The voice spoke, solemn and resonant.

"Behold the age of wickedness, when the thoughts of humanity were only evil continually."

Peter's gaze turned toward the heavens, where the cries of the innocent rose like smoke, mingling with the groans of the earth itself. The very fabric of creation seemed strained under the weight of humanity's sin. Violence, greed, and lust dominated the land, and the memory of the Creator had all but vanished from their hearts.

In the midst of this darkness, Peter was shown one man who stood apart, a beacon of righteousness in a world gone astray.

"This is Noah," the voice said. "A man blameless in his generation, who walked with God when all others turned away."

Peter saw Noah, a simple yet steadfast figure, kneeling in prayer beside an altar of unhewn stone. His face bore the marks of age and toil, but his eyes reflected a deep and abiding faith. Around him were his family—his wife, sons, and daughters-in-law—who shared in his devotion.

The voice continued. "To Noah I revealed my sorrow and my plan. For the earth is filled with violence through humanity, and behold, I will destroy them with the earth."

Peter's heart ached at the gravity of the words, yet he saw in Noah a determination born of trust in the Creator's justice and mercy.

Peter watched as Noah received divine instruction to build an ark. The vision revealed the enormity of the task—a massive vessel of gopher wood, its dimensions and design dictated by the Creator Himself. It was a refuge, a testament to God's mercy amidst His judgment.

Noah and his family labored tirelessly, enduring the scorn and mockery of their neighbors. Peter saw the jeering crowds, their laughter a bitter contrast to the steadfast resolve of the righteous man.

"Why do you build this folly?" they taunted. "The heavens have not opened, and the earth is unshaken. Your God has forgotten you!"

Yet Noah did not waver. Guided by faith, he completed the ark, knowing that obedience to God was more valuable than the approval of men.

As the ark stood ready, Peter was shown a miraculous gathering of animals, two by two and seven by seven, as prescribed. Birds of every color, beasts of all sizes, and creeping things of the earth entered the ark, as though guided by an unseen hand.

The scene shifted, and the voice spoke again. "Then the fountains of the great deep burst forth, and the windows of the heavens were opened."

Rain began to fall—softly at first, then in torrents. The ground quaked, and waters erupted from beneath, swallowing the land. The people who had mocked Noah now ran in terror, their cries for deliverance rising too late.

Peter saw the earth transform into a vast, unbroken sea, where only the ark remained afloat. It carried within it the seed of a new beginning, a covenant preserved through Noah's faithfulness.

The vision lingered upon the waters, where the ark drifted for forty days and forty nights. Inside, Noah and his family endured in faith, trusting that the God who brought the flood would also bring them safely to dry ground.

Peter was shown the moment when the rains ceased, and the waters began to recede. Mountains emerged, their peaks breaking through the surface like islands of hope. The ark came to rest upon the mountains of Ararat, and Noah sent forth a dove to find dry land.

The bird returned with an olive leaf, a symbol of peace and restoration. Peter's heart swelled at the sight, understanding that even in judgment, God's mercy endured.

The vision then turned to the aftermath of the flood. Noah and his family stepped onto the cleansed earth, their feet sinking into the damp soil of a world reborn. They built an altar and offered sacrifices to God, their prayers mingling with the aroma of the offering.

The voice spoke, filled with promise. "Never again will I curse the ground because of man, nor will I destroy every living creature as I have done. I establish my covenant with you and your descendants, and with every living creature that is with you."

Peter saw the sign of this covenant—a brilliant rainbow arching across the sky, its colors radiant and eternal. It was a symbol of hope, a reminder that the Creator's judgment was always tempered by His love.

As Peter emerged from the vision, the weight of what he had seen pressed upon him. The flood was not merely an act of destruction but a profound act of cleansing and renewal. It was a reminder of humanity's capacity for wickedness and the enduring mercy of God.

Peter shared the vision with those who would listen, speaking of Noah's faith and the covenant that God established with all living things.

"The flood was a warning," he said, "but also a promise. God's mercy is vast, yet His justice cannot be denied. Let us walk in righteousness, as Noah did, and trust in the faithfulness of the Creator."

His words stirred the hearts of his listeners, some moved to repentance and others inspired by the enduring promise of the rainbow. Yet Peter knew that the lessons of the flood were not just for his generation but for all who would follow.

The story of Noah and the flood became a cornerstone of his testimony, a call to faithfulness in the face of a world prone to corruption. Through it, Peter reminded humanity of the delicate balance between judgment and grace—a balance that rested not in the hands of men, but in the heart of the Creator.

Chapter 8
The Tower of Babel

The vision carried Peter to a vast plain, where the horizon stretched endlessly beneath a sky of piercing clarity. Before him rose a structure of unimaginable scale, its foundations embedded deeply into the earth and its summit lost in the heavens. The Tower of Babel, a monument to human ambition, stood defiant against the order of creation.

"This," the voice intoned, "is the arrogance of humanity, who sought to reach the heavens by their own strength."

Peter stood at the base of the tower, surrounded by a throng of people. They worked tirelessly, their faces set with determination and pride. From the top of the tower, the sounds of chisels and hammers echoed as the edifice climbed ever higher. The atmosphere was charged with a sense of unity, but it was not a unity born of righteousness.

"They have become one in rebellion," the voice continued. "Their unity serves not to glorify the Creator but to defy Him."

The story began in the aftermath of the flood. Humanity, having survived judgment, spread across the earth, their numbers growing once more. But as they multiplied, so too did their pride. Peter was shown their decision to settle in the land of Shinar, where fertile soil and abundant resources promised prosperity.

"We will build a city for ourselves," the people declared, "and a tower with its top in the heavens. Let us make a name for ourselves, lest we be scattered across the face of the earth."

Their words revealed their intent. The city was not for refuge or worship but as a declaration of their independence from the Creator. The tower was their rebellion made manifest—a physical attempt to claim the heavens as their own.

Peter observed the construction, marveling at its complexity. The people worked with an efficiency born of shared purpose, using bricks baked in fire and mortar made from bitumen. Their knowledge and ingenuity were remarkable, but their hearts were far from God.

The vision shifted, revealing the spiritual impact of their endeavor. Peter saw how their unity and ambition, though impressive on the surface, were tainted by pride and fear. The tower was not a symbol of hope but of defiance, a monument to the belief that humanity could control its destiny without the Creator.

"They seek to ascend by their own strength," the voice said, "but the heavens cannot be reached through pride. Their hearts are closed to me, and their labor will end in ruin."

As Peter gazed upward, he felt the weight of the tower's defiance. Its shadow stretched across the plain, a stark reminder of humanity's tendency to exalt itself above the divine.

Then came the intervention of the Almighty. Peter was shown a gathering in the heavens, where the Creator spoke with the authority of infinite wisdom.

"Behold, they are one people, and they have one language. This is only the beginning of what they will do. Let us go down and confuse their language, so they may not understand one another."

Peter trembled as he witnessed the divine descent. The once harmonious voices of the builders became a cacophony of confusion. Men and women shouted at one another, their words incomprehensible, their coordination unraveling. The tools fell silent, and the great tower stood unfinished, its stones a testament to the futility of rebellion.

The people, no longer able to communicate, scattered across the earth, their dream of unity shattered.

Peter's vision lingered on the aftermath of Babel. The once-thriving plain became desolate, the city abandoned, and the tower crumbling under the weight of time. Yet even in the ruins, Peter saw the mercy of God.

The confusion of languages was not merely an act of judgment but a means to preserve humanity from greater harm. By scattering the people, the Creator ensured that their unity in rebellion would not lead to their complete destruction.

"This," the voice explained, "is both judgment and grace. I will not abandon humanity, but I will not allow them to destroy themselves in their pride."

When Peter returned to his earthly surroundings, he pondered the lessons of Babel. The story was not merely about a tower but about the dangers of human arrogance and the consequences of seeking greatness apart from God.

He shared the vision with those who would listen, speaking of the folly of the builders and the wisdom of the Creator.

"The tower reached high," Peter said, "but it was built on a foundation of pride. Let us remember that true greatness lies not in exalting ourselves, but in humbling ourselves before God."

Peter's words resonated with his listeners. Some were reminded of their own ambitions, recognizing the subtle ways in which pride had crept into their lives. Others found hope in the reminder that God's judgment was always tempered by mercy.

Through his testimony, Peter emphasized the need for humility and dependence on the Creator. He urged his listeners to seek unity not in rebellion but in righteousness, to build not monuments to themselves but lives that glorified God.

The story of Babel became a cornerstone of Peter's teaching, a warning against the dangers of pride and the importance of walking in obedience. And as he continued to proclaim the vision, he prayed that humanity would learn from the past, choosing the path of humility and faithfulness over the empty pursuit of self-exaltation.

Chapter 9
Sodom and Gomorrah

Peter's vision descended upon him like a weighty shadow, enveloping his senses and transporting him to a land that shimmered with wealth and beauty but hid a deep and festering darkness. The cities of Sodom and Gomorrah rose before him, their gates bustling with activity, their streets lined with the opulence of a prosperous people. Yet beneath the veneer of abundance, a corruption thrived that would soon draw divine wrath upon them.

"This," the voice said, resonant with sorrow and justice, "is the end of a people who have turned their backs on righteousness."

Peter stood at the edge of Sodom, his spirit trembling as he observed its inhabitants. They moved about their lives with apparent joy, yet their deeds were steeped in arrogance, cruelty, and unbridled indulgence. The cries of the oppressed and the violated rose from the heart of the city, mingling with the acrid smoke of sacrifices made not to the Creator but to idols of their own making.

The vision drew Peter deeper, revealing the nature of Sodom's sin. Its people had abandoned the Creator's ways, rejecting justice and mercy in favor of self-gratification. Peter saw acts of violence and perversion in the open streets, a society in which the weak were trampled and the stranger was despised.

Yet amid the darkness, there was a flicker of light. Peter was shown the household of Lot, a man who sought to live righteously despite the corruption around him. Lot's face was weary, his spirit burdened by the wickedness that surrounded him, but his faith remained intact.

The voice spoke again. "For the sake of one righteous man, I delayed my judgment, but the time has come, for the outcry against these cities is great, and their sin is very grievous."

Peter was then transported to a pivotal moment. Three figures, radiant and otherworldly, approached the city. They bore the unmistakable presence of messengers sent by the Almighty. Peter recognized one of them as the Lord Himself, cloaked in a form that humanity could endure.

The vision shifted to a hill overlooking the plain, where Abraham, the patriarch, stood in earnest prayer. He pleaded for the cities, his voice filled with compassion and concern.

"Will you sweep away the righteous with the wicked?" Abraham asked. "Far be it from you to do such a thing! Shall not the Judge of all the earth do what is just?"

The Lord's response was both patient and just. "If I find ten righteous people in the city, I will spare it for their sake."

Peter's heart ached as he realized the gravity of the moment. The mercy of God was vast, but the wickedness of Sodom and Gomorrah was too great.

As night fell, Peter was shown the final hours of Sodom. Lot welcomed the heavenly messengers into his home, offering them shelter and protection. But the city's wickedness soon revealed itself. A mob gathered at Lot's door, demanding that the strangers be handed over to them for their vile purposes.

Lot, desperate to protect his guests, stepped outside, pleading with the crowd. His voice trembled as he begged them to turn away from their evil. But their hearts were hardened, their lust and violence unchecked.

The messengers intervened, pulling Lot back inside and striking the mob with blindness. "Gather your family," they urged him. "Flee this place, for the Lord is about to destroy the city."

Peter saw Lot's desperate attempt to save his family. He pleaded with his sons-in-law, urging them to leave with him, but they laughed, dismissing his warning as the ravings of a madman. With heavy hearts, Lot, his wife, and his two daughters fled the city, guided by the messengers.

The vision shifted again, and Peter was shown the destruction of Sodom and Gomorrah. Fire and brimstone rained down from the heavens, consuming everything in their path. The once-thriving cities were reduced to smoldering ruins, their wickedness erased from the earth.

Lot's wife, unable to leave the life she had known behind, turned back despite the warning. Peter saw her transformed into a pillar of salt, a somber monument to the danger of clinging to the past.

The aftermath of the destruction was a scene of desolation. The lush plain, once likened to the garden of the Lord, became a barren wasteland. Smoke rose from the ashes, a stark reminder of the consequences of unrepentant sin.

Yet even in the midst of judgment, Peter saw the mercy of God. Lot and his daughters found refuge in the mountains, their lives spared because of their faithfulness. The vision lingered on Lot's tear-streaked face as he prayed, his heart heavy with both gratitude and sorrow.

When Peter returned from the vision, he felt the weight of its lessons pressing upon him. The story of Sodom and Gomorrah was not merely a tale of destruction but a profound warning about the dangers of turning away from righteousness and rejecting the ways of the Creator.

He shared the vision with those around him, his voice filled with urgency. "The sins of Sodom were not hidden from the Lord, nor are ours. Let us not grow complacent in our ways, for His justice is sure. Yet His mercy endures for those who repent and seek Him."

Peter's words stirred both fear and hope among his listeners. Some recognized their own failings and resolved to change their ways. Others marveled at the mercy of God, who spared the righteous even in the midst of judgment.

Through his testimony, Peter reminded humanity of the balance between divine justice and mercy. The story of Sodom and Gomorrah became a cornerstone of his teaching, a call to repentance and a plea to seek righteousness in a world that so often turns away from the light.

And as he continued to proclaim the vision, Peter prayed that the lessons of the cities would not be forgotten, but would inspire all who heard them to walk humbly with their God.

Chapter 10
The Exodus

The vision opened with the crackling heat of the desert sun, its unrelenting glare illuminating the vast expanse of Egypt's land. Peter found himself standing amidst a multitude of people, their faces marked by weariness and despair. These were the descendants of Abraham, Isaac, and Jacob—the children of Israel—enslaved under the harsh rule of Pharaoh. The sounds of their toil filled the air: the clatter of bricks, the lash of whips, and the muffled cries of a people burdened by generations of oppression.

The voice came to Peter, resonant and filled with both sorrow and resolve. "Behold, my people are in bondage. Their cries have reached my ears, and I have remembered my covenant with Abraham."

Peter's vision shifted to the wilderness, where a solitary figure stood before a bush engulfed in flames yet unconsumed. This was Moses, the reluctant shepherd chosen by God to deliver His people. Peter watched as the voice of the Almighty spoke from the fire, commanding Moses to return to Egypt and confront Pharaoh with a divine demand.

"Go and tell Pharaoh," the voice declared, "to let my people go, that they may serve me."

Peter saw the struggle in Moses' heart, the fear and doubt that clouded his resolve. But the Creator reassured him, granting signs and wonders to confirm His authority. With a staff that turned to a serpent and a hand that became leprous and was healed, Moses was armed not with weapons, but with the power of God.

The vision carried Peter to the courts of Pharaoh, where Moses and his brother Aaron stood before the mighty ruler of Egypt. Pharaoh, draped in opulent robes and seated on a gilded throne, listened with a mix of disdain and amusement as Moses delivered the command of the Lord.

"Thus says the Lord, the God of Israel: Let my people go, that they may hold a feast to me in the wilderness."

Pharaoh's laughter was cold, his voice dripping with arrogance. "Who is the Lord, that I should obey His voice? I do not know the Lord, and moreover, I will not let Israel go."

Peter saw the hardening of Pharaoh's heart as the plagues began to descend upon Egypt. Each plague was a direct challenge to the gods of the Egyptians, a demonstration of the Creator's supremacy over their false idols.

Peter witnessed the waters of the Nile turning to blood, the lifeblood of Egypt becoming a symbol of judgment. Frogs swarmed the land, followed by gnats and flies, each plague more devastating than the last. Livestock perished, boils afflicted the people, and hail rained down with fire, destroying crops and homes alike.

Yet Pharaoh remained unyielding, his pride blinding him to the power of the Almighty. Even as locusts devoured what little remained, and darkness fell over the land for three days, Pharaoh's heart remained hardened.

Peter's spirit grieved as he saw the suffering of the Egyptians, the innocent caught in the wake of their ruler's defiance. But he also understood the justice of the Lord, who was not only judging Pharaoh but fulfilling His promise to deliver His people.

The vision reached its climax with the final plague—the death of the firstborn. Peter stood among the Israelites as they prepared for the night of deliverance, each family selecting a spotless lamb and marking their doorposts with its blood.

"This is the Passover," the voice said. "When I see the blood, I will pass over you, and no plague shall fall upon you to destroy you."

Peter saw the solemnity of the moment as the Israelites ate the Passover meal in haste, their sandals on their feet and staffs in their hands, ready to leave at a moment's notice. The cries of Egypt filled the night as the angel of death passed through the land, striking down the firstborn of every household that was not marked by the blood.

Pharaoh, broken by the loss of his own son, finally relented. "Go," he said to Moses, his voice trembling with grief. "Take your people and leave."

The vision carried Peter to the Red Sea, where the Israelites found themselves pursued by Pharaoh's army, his heart hardened once more. Trapped between the sea and the chariots of Egypt, fear gripped the people, but Moses stood firm.

"Fear not," he declared, "stand firm, and see the salvation of the Lord, which He will work for you today."

Peter watched in awe as Moses stretched out his staff over the sea, and the waters parted, revealing dry ground. The Israelites crossed safely, the walls of water towering on either side. When Pharaoh's army followed, the sea returned to its place, engulfing the chariots and horsemen in a final act of judgment.

On the far side of the sea, Peter saw the Israelites lift their voices in a song of triumph. Miriam, the sister of Moses, led the women in dancing, tambourines in hand, singing, "Sing to the Lord, for He has triumphed gloriously; the horse and his rider He has thrown into the sea."

Yet even in the midst of celebration, Peter sensed the challenges that lay ahead. The wilderness awaited, a time of testing that would reveal the hearts of the people.

When Peter returned from the vision, his heart was heavy with the weight of its meaning. The story of the Exodus was not just a tale of deliverance but a testament to the power of God's faithfulness and the dangers of human pride.

He shared the vision with those who would listen, his voice filled with both awe and urgency. "The Lord hears the cries of His people," Peter said. "He is faithful to deliver, but He also calls us to obedience and trust. Let us not harden our hearts as Pharaoh did, but follow Him with humility and faith."

Peter's words stirred his listeners, inspiring them to reflect on their own lives. Some found hope in the reminder that God is a deliverer, while others were challenged to examine the hardness of their hearts.

Through his testimony, Peter reminded humanity of the lessons of the Exodus—a call to trust in the Lord's provision and to walk faithfully in His ways. The story of the Israelites' journey from slavery to freedom became a cornerstone of his teaching, a reminder of the enduring covenant between God and His people.

And as he continued to proclaim the vision, Peter prayed that all who heard would find their own exodus, leaving behind the bondage of sin and walking in the freedom of the Creator's love.

Chapter 11
Mosaic Law

The vision carried Peter to the base of a mountain wreathed in cloud and fire, its peak obscured by the radiance of divine glory. The air was charged with a holiness so palpable that Peter trembled in awe. Around him, a multitude of people stood at a distance, their faces marked by a mixture of reverence and fear.

"This is Sinai," the voice said, resonating like the thunder that rolled across the heavens. "Here, I revealed my covenant to a chosen people, that they might walk in my ways."

Peter's gaze turned to a single figure ascending the mountain—Moses, the man called to mediate between God and His people. Clad in humility and courage, Moses climbed higher, disappearing into the cloud of glory that rested upon the summit. The people below watched in silence, the fire and smoke a reminder of the holiness they dared not approach.

As Peter followed in spirit, he saw Moses enter the presence of the Almighty. The voice spoke to Moses, each word imbued with power and love, a revelation of divine will.

"I am the Lord your God, who brought you out of the land of Egypt, out of the house of slavery. You shall have no other gods before me."

The commandments were given, each one a foundation for a life of righteousness and justice. Peter felt their weight, not as burdens but as gifts—guidelines that reflected the character of the Creator and His desire for humanity to live in harmony with Him and one another.

The vision shifted, and Peter saw Moses descending the mountain, his arms bearing two stone tablets engraved by the finger of God. The people, impatient in his absence, had turned to idolatry, crafting a golden calf and proclaiming it their god. Their revelry was a bitter contrast to the sanctity of the covenant Moses carried.

Peter's heart ached as he watched Moses confront the people, his face radiant with the glory of God but his spirit heavy with righteous anger. The tablets, symbols of the covenant, shattered against the ground, reflecting the brokenness of the people's relationship with their Creator.

Yet even in the midst of judgment, there was mercy. Moses returned to the mountain, interceding on behalf of the people. The voice responded with both justice and grace, renewing the covenant and engraving the commandments once more.

The vision broadened, revealing the full scope of the Mosaic Law. Peter saw its many facets—the moral laws that called for righteousness, the ceremonial laws that guided worship, and the civil laws that ensured justice among the people. Each law was a thread in the tapestry of the covenant, weaving together a picture of a holy and just society.

"This is my covenant," the voice said, "not to burden, but to bless; not to enslave, but to set free."

Peter was shown how the law set Israel apart, a people consecrated to the Creator amidst the nations of the earth. The festivals and sacrifices, the Sabbaths and rituals, all pointed to a deeper truth—the need for atonement and the promise of redemption.

As Peter watched, he was shown the limitations of the law. Though perfect in its intent, it could not change the hearts of those who followed it. He saw the people stumble time and again, their obedience faltering, their faith waning.

The voice spoke again, its tone filled with both lament and hope. "The law is holy, but the hearts of men are weak. It is a shadow of what is to come, a guide that points to the fulfillment of the covenant in my Son."

Peter's spirit trembled as he glimpsed the connection between the law and the promise of the Messiah. The sacrifices of lambs and goats, the blood sprinkled on the altar, all foreshadowed the ultimate sacrifice that would bring true and lasting atonement.

The vision shifted once more, and Peter saw the people of Israel wandering in the wilderness, their journey guided by the pillar of cloud by day and fire by night. Despite their grumbling and rebellion, the Creator's presence remained with them, a testament to His enduring faithfulness.

At the heart of their camp stood the tabernacle, a portable sanctuary where heaven and earth met. Peter was shown the intricate design of the tabernacle, its golden ark and sacred furnishings, each element a reflection of divine glory.

"This is where I dwell among my people," the voice said, "a shadow of the greater dwelling to come."

When Peter returned from the vision, his heart burned with understanding. The Mosaic Law was not merely a set of rules but a revelation of God's holiness and His desire for humanity to walk in fellowship with Him.

He shared the vision with those who would listen, speaking of the commandments and the covenant, the sacrifices and the tabernacle.

"The law reveals the character of God," Peter said. "It is a lamp to guide our feet, but it also shows us our need for grace. Let us honor the law, not by works alone, but by turning our hearts to the One who fulfills it."

Peter's words resonated deeply, inspiring his listeners to reflect on their own lives. Some were moved to repentance, recognizing their inability to fulfill the law on their own. Others found hope in the promise of the Messiah, who would bring the law to completion.

Through his testimony, Peter emphasized the enduring relevance of the Mosaic Law—not as a burden, but as a guide that leads to the greater covenant of grace. The story of Mount Sinai and the giving of the law became a cornerstone of his teaching, a reminder of the holiness of God and His unyielding desire for relationship with His people.

And as Peter continued to proclaim the vision, he prayed that all who heard would find in the law not condemnation, but the promise of redemption through the One who came to fulfill it.

Chapter 12
The Prophets

The vision drew Peter into the heart of ancient Israel, where the land lay vibrant and alive, yet burdened by the weight of its people's rebellion. The winds carried whispers of divine warnings, interwoven with promises of hope. Peter found himself in the presence of men and women who stood apart, chosen by the Creator to deliver His words to a wayward nation. These were the prophets, the watchmen of Israel, whose voices carried both thunder and solace.

"These are my messengers," the voice declared, resonant with both authority and tenderness. "They speak not their own words, but mine. Through them, I call my people to return to me."

Peter first saw Elijah, the fiery prophet of Mount Carmel. He stood alone before the prophets of Baal, his figure commanding and unyielding. Around him gathered a nation torn between loyalty to the God of their ancestors and the seductive allure of foreign idols.

"How long will you go limping between two opinions?" Elijah cried. "If the Lord is God, follow Him; but if Baal, then follow him."

Peter witnessed the dramatic showdown as Elijah prayed, and fire fell from heaven, consuming the sacrifice, the altar, and even the water surrounding it. The people fell on their faces, crying, "The Lord, He is God!"

Yet, even in his triumph, Peter saw Elijah's anguish, fleeing into the wilderness and lamenting his isolation. The Creator's response came not in fire or storm, but in a gentle whisper, reminding Elijah that he was never truly alone.

The vision shifted, and Peter was shown Isaiah, whose words soared like poetry yet struck with the force of a hammer. Standing before a vision of the Lord, high and lifted up, Isaiah cried out, "Woe is me! For I am lost; for I am a man of unclean lips, and I dwell in the midst of a people of unclean lips."

Peter watched as a seraphim touched a burning coal to Isaiah's lips, cleansing him and preparing him for his mission. Isaiah's prophecies painted a dual picture—of judgment for sin and rebellion, but also of the coming Messiah, the Suffering Servant who would bear the iniquities of humanity.

"By His wounds we are healed," Isaiah declared, and Peter's heart burned with the recognition of his Master in those words.

Next, Peter stood with Jeremiah, the weeping prophet, whose heart broke for the people of Judah. Peter saw him pleading with kings and priests, warning of the impending exile if they did not turn from their wicked ways.

"This is the covenant I will make with the house of Israel," Jeremiah proclaimed, his voice trembling with both sorrow and hope. "I will put my law within them, and I will write it on their hearts. And I will be their God, and they shall be my people."

Peter felt the weight of Jeremiah's sorrow as he was mocked, imprisoned, and cast into a cistern. Yet Jeremiah's faith remained steadfast, sustained by the promise of restoration and a new covenant.

Ezekiel came into view, a prophet of visions and symbols. Peter saw the valley of dry bones, a desolate expanse where death reigned. Ezekiel stood amidst the bones, and the voice of the Creator commanded, "Prophesy over these bones, and say to them, O dry bones, hear the word of the Lord."

As Ezekiel spoke, Peter watched in awe as the bones rattled, came together, and were clothed with flesh. Breath entered them, and they stood as a vast army—a vision of resurrection and the restoration of God's people.

The voice spoke to Peter, explaining, "My prophets spoke not only of judgment but of renewal. They proclaimed that death would not have the final word, for I am the God of life."

Peter was then shown the smaller voices, the so-called minor prophets, whose messages carried no less weight. Amos decried injustice, calling for rivers of righteousness to flow. Hosea's life became a living parable of God's unwavering love for His unfaithful people. Micah spoke of walking humbly with God, and Malachi foretold the coming of Elijah before the great and terrible day of the Lord.

Each prophet, in their time and place, bore the burden of speaking truth to a people often unwilling to listen. Yet their words endured, preserved as a testament to the Creator's unrelenting pursuit of His people.

As the vision drew to a close, Peter saw a golden thread running through the lives of the prophets—a thread of hope, woven into the fabric of their warnings and promises. It pointed toward the coming of the Messiah, the fulfillment of the covenant, and the restoration of all things.

The voice spoke one final time. "My prophets were voices crying in the wilderness, preparing the way for my Son. Their message endures, calling all who hear to repentance and hope."

When Peter returned from the vision, his heart was heavy with the weight of the prophets' words but also filled with the hope they carried. He gathered the faithful and shared what he had seen.

"The prophets were not sent to destroy but to restore," Peter said. "Their warnings were born of love, and their promises spoke of redemption. Let us heed their voices, for they call us back to the God who longs to be our Father."

Peter's testimony stirred a deep response among his listeners. Some reflected on the warnings of the prophets, recognizing the need for repentance in their own lives. Others were inspired by the promises, finding hope in the assurance of God's faithfulness.

Through his words, Peter emphasized the enduring relevance of the prophets. Their messages were not relics of the past but living words that continued to speak to the hearts of humanity.

And as Peter proclaimed the vision, he prayed that all who heard would respond to the prophets' call, turning from their sin and embracing the hope of the restoration to come.

Chapter 13
The Messiah

The vision unfolded with a radiance unlike any Peter had seen before. A light pierced the darkness, illuminating the breadth of human history. At the center of this brilliance stood the figure of the Messiah, the promised one foretold by prophets and longed for by generations. Peter felt his spirit tremble with awe as he beheld the fulfillment of divine promise embodied in one man.

"This is my Son," the voice said, resonant with love and authority. "In Him, all my promises are fulfilled, and through Him, the hope of humanity is restored."

Peter was transported to the town of Bethlehem on a quiet night under a canopy of stars. He saw shepherds keeping watch over their flocks, their lives marked by simplicity and toil. Suddenly, the heavens burst open, and an angel appeared, proclaiming, "Fear not, for behold, I bring you good news of great joy that will be for all the people. For unto you is born this day in the city of David a Savior, who is Christ the Lord."

The shepherds hurried to a stable, where they found the infant Messiah lying in a manger, His presence humble yet divine. Peter's heart swelled at the sight, understanding that the Creator had chosen to enter the world not in power and grandeur, but in humility and vulnerability.

"This is how I love the world," the voice explained. "Through my Son, I dwell among my people, bringing salvation to the lowly and the lost."

The vision shifted, carrying Peter through the life of the Messiah. He saw Him as a child in the temple, astonishing the teachers with His understanding and wisdom. He witnessed the moment of His baptism in the Jordan, where the heavens opened and the Spirit descended like a dove, and the voice of the Almighty declared, "This is my beloved Son, with whom I am well pleased."

Peter followed the Messiah through towns and villages, where He healed the sick, gave sight to the blind, and cast out demons. He saw crowds gather to hear His teachings, their faces filled with wonder as He spoke of the kingdom of heaven, forgiveness, and the love of God.

"This is the fulfillment of the law and the prophets," the voice said. "In my Son, the broken are made whole, the lost are found, and the weary find rest."

Yet the vision also revealed the rejection the Messiah faced. Peter saw the leaders of Israel, their hearts hardened by pride and fear, conspiring against Him. He watched as the crowds, once eager to hear His words, turned away, unable to accept the cost of discipleship.

The voice spoke again, filled with sorrow. "He was despised and rejected by men, a man of sorrows and acquainted with grief. Yet through His suffering, He brings redemption."

Peter's spirit ached as the vision carried him to Jerusalem, where the Messiah entered the city to shouts of "Hosanna!" only to face betrayal and condemnation days later.

The vision lingered on the night of the Last Supper, where the Messiah gathered with His disciples. Peter saw himself in the room, his heart filled with both devotion and confusion. The Messiah broke bread and shared the cup, declaring, "This is my body, given for you. This cup is the new covenant in my blood, poured out for many for the forgiveness of sins."

Peter understood now what he had struggled to grasp in that moment: the Messiah's mission was not to conquer through power, but to save through sacrifice.

The vision turned somber as it revealed the path to Golgotha. Peter saw the Messiah, beaten and bloodied, carrying His cross through the streets of Jerusalem. The crowd jeered, yet among them were those who wept, their sorrow a testament to their love for Him.

At the place of the skull, Peter witnessed the crucifixion—the nails driven into flesh, the agonizing cries, and the darkness that fell over the land. The Messiah's final words echoed through the vision: "It is finished."

The earth quaked, and the veil of the temple was torn in two, signifying that the barrier between God and humanity had been removed.

But the vision did not end in death. Peter was transported to the garden tomb, where the stone had been rolled away. He saw the risen Messiah, radiant with the glory of victory over sin and death. The wounds in His hands and side were visible, yet they no longer signified pain but triumph.

"This is the hope of humanity," the voice declared. "Through my Son, death is defeated, and life eternal is offered to all who believe."

Peter's heart burned with understanding as the vision faded. The Messiah was not just a figure of the past but the living fulfillment of all that had been promised. His life, death, and resurrection were the cornerstone of humanity's redemption, the bridge between the Creator and His creation.

Peter gathered the faithful and shared the vision with urgency and joy.

"The Messiah has come," he proclaimed. "He is the hope of the nations, the light of the world, and the fulfillment of God's promise. In Him, we find life, and through Him, we are restored."

Peter's testimony moved his listeners deeply. Some wept with gratitude, recognizing the Messiah as their Savior. Others, burdened by guilt, found hope in the assurance of forgiveness.

Through his words, Peter emphasized the centrality of the Messiah to the divine plan. His coming was not just an event in history but the fulfillment of a covenant that stretched from eternity past to eternity future.

And as Peter continued to proclaim the vision, he prayed that all who heard would embrace the Messiah, finding in Him the redemption and hope that only He could offer.

Chapter 14
The Cross

The vision opened with a stark and haunting clarity, drawing Peter to the foot of a rugged hill outside Jerusalem. The place, called Golgotha, stood as a grim silhouette against a storm-darkened sky. At its summit were three crosses, stark and imposing, their wooden frames stained with the blood of those condemned.

"This is the center of my plan," the voice said, its tone both somber and triumphant. "Here, justice and mercy meet, and the fate of all humanity is decided."

Peter's spirit trembled as he approached the central cross, where the Messiah hung in agony. His body was broken, His face marred beyond recognition, and yet a profound peace radiated from Him. Peter was struck by the paradox of the scene: the Savior of the world, abandoned and humiliated, bearing the weight of sin upon His shoulders.

The crowd below was a mixture of scorn and sorrow. Some mocked, their voices filled with disdain: "If you are the Son of God, come down from the cross!" Others wept silently, their hearts breaking at the sight of the innocent Lamb suffering for the guilty.

Above the cross was a sign, written in multiple languages: **"Jesus of Nazareth, King of the Jews."** It was meant as a mockery, but Peter now understood its truth. The cross was not a defeat—it was a coronation, the ultimate act of kingship.

The vision drew Peter into the spiritual significance of the moment. He saw the Messiah's suffering not as the result of human cruelty alone but as the deliberate fulfillment of divine justice. The sins of humanity, from the smallest deceit to the gravest atrocity, were placed upon Him.

"This is the cup He chose to drink," the voice said. "The wrath reserved for the guilty is poured out upon the innocent, that the guilty may go free."

Peter was shown the darkness that enveloped the earth, a manifestation of the separation the Messiah endured. He heard the piercing cry: "My God, my God, why have you forsaken me?" It was the cry of one who bore the full weight of humanity's estrangement from the Creator.

The vision shifted to reveal the spiritual realm, where forces of darkness had gathered, believing they had won. Peter saw them reveling in their apparent triumph, unaware that their defeat was imminent. The cross, a symbol of shame and death, was becoming the instrument of their undoing.

"This is the mystery of redemption," the voice explained. "Through death, life is restored. Through suffering, victory is achieved. Through the cross, my love is made complete."

Peter watched as the Messiah's final words echoed through both the physical and spiritual realms: "It is finished." At that moment, the veil of the temple was torn in two, from top to bottom, symbolizing the removal of the barrier between God and humanity.

The vision lingered at the foot of the cross, where Peter saw a small group of faithful followers—Mary, the mother of Jesus; John, the beloved disciple; and Mary Magdalene. Their faces were marked by grief, but within their sorrow was an unshakable love.

The Messiah's body was taken down, wrapped in linen, and placed in a tomb. A heavy stone was rolled across the entrance, sealing what seemed to be the end of hope. But Peter now knew what the others could not yet see: the cross was not the end, but the beginning of a new covenant, sealed by the blood of the Lamb.

The vision expanded, revealing the ripple effect of the cross through time and space. Peter saw countless souls kneeling in repentance, their burdens lifted as they placed their faith in the one who had died for them. He saw lives transformed, chains of sin broken, and relationships restored.

"This is the power of the cross," the voice said. "It is foolishness to those who are perishing, but to those who are being saved, it is the power of God."

Peter's spirit soared as he witnessed the triumph of the cross. The Messiah's sacrifice was not a one-time event, but an eternal act of love, drawing all who would believe into the embrace of the Creator.

When the vision faded, Peter felt the weight of the cross pressing upon his soul. It was not a burden of sorrow, but a profound understanding of its significance. The cross was the fulcrum of history, the place where sin was defeated, and grace was unleashed.

He gathered the faithful and spoke of what he had seen, his voice trembling with both grief and joy.

"The cross is the heart of our faith," Peter declared. "It is where the love of God and the justice of God meet. Through it, we are reconciled to the Father, and through it, we are called to live in His grace."

Peter's words stirred the hearts of his listeners. Some wept openly, overwhelmed by the magnitude of the sacrifice. Others knelt in silence, their spirits lifted by the hope the cross offered.

Through his testimony, Peter emphasized the centrality of the cross to the divine plan. It was not merely a symbol of suffering but the ultimate expression of love, a call to surrender and trust in the one who gave everything for humanity.

And as Peter continued to proclaim the vision, he prayed that all who heard would come to the foot of the cross, laying down their burdens and receiving the life that flowed from the sacrifice of the Messiah.

Chapter 15
The Tree of Life

The vision opened with a radiant light that pierced through the mists of eternity, drawing Peter to the heart of a garden more beautiful than any place he had ever seen. This was not an ordinary garden; it was Eden reborn, a realm where the fullness of life and divine communion flourished. At the center stood the Tree of Life, its trunk immense and its branches stretching outward as though to embrace all creation.

"This is the symbol of eternal life," the voice said, its tone filled with both reverence and promise. "In it is the essence of my covenant with humanity."

Peter's gaze was drawn to the tree's fruit, which glowed with a light that seemed alive, pulsing gently as if it contained the heartbeat of the Creator Himself. The leaves shimmered like emeralds, their edges sparkling as though touched by dew from the river that flowed at the base of the tree.

In this place, the air carried a purity that Peter had never experienced before. It was more than just the absence of corruption; it was the presence of perfect harmony. Every sound, every scent, every movement seemed to join in a symphony of life that centered on the Tree of Life.

The vision shifted, and Peter was taken back to the beginning, to the first garden where the Tree of Life had originally stood. He saw Adam and Eve walking freely, their faces radiant with innocence and joy. They moved in unbroken fellowship with the Creator, the tree a testament to the eternal life they were meant to enjoy.

But then Peter saw the shadow of the other tree—the Tree of the Knowledge of Good and Evil. He witnessed the serpent, cunning and deceitful, weaving his lies into the hearts of humanity. The choice to disobey was made, and Peter felt the shattering of the harmony that had once filled the garden.

The voice spoke, heavy with sorrow. "The way to the Tree of Life was barred, for humanity had chosen death over life. Yet even in their fall, I planted the seed of redemption."

Peter was shown the flaming sword and the cherubim guarding the way to the tree. It was a barrier of both judgment and mercy—a protection that kept humanity from reaching out to take eternal life in their corrupted state.

The vision leaped forward through the ages, showing Peter how the longing for the Tree of Life had persisted in the hearts of humanity. He saw its shadow in the stories of many cultures, its promise whispered in the prophecies of the Scriptures.

"Life eternal is not forgotten," the voice said. "What was lost in Eden will be restored in my kingdom."

The vision shifted once more, and Peter was transported to the New Jerusalem. The Tree of Life stood again at the center, its roots nourished by the River of Life that flowed from the throne of God and the Lamb. Its fruit, abundant and diverse, was available to all who dwelled in the city.

Peter saw multitudes gathered around the tree, their faces shining with peace and joy. The nations of the earth were healed, and the tree's leaves became a balm for every wound, a cure for every sorrow.

"There is no longer any curse," the voice said. "For my Son has borne it, and the way to the Tree of Life is open to all who believe."

Peter was shown how the Tree of Life represented more than just physical immortality. It was a symbol of eternal communion with the Creator, a restoration of the relationship that had been broken in Eden. Through the sacrifice of the Messiah, the barriers had been removed, and the invitation to partake of the tree was extended to all.

"This is my promise," the voice declared. "To him who overcomes, I will give the right to eat from the Tree of Life, which is in the paradise of God."

As the vision faded, Peter returned to the earthly realm, his heart ablaze with the hope of what he had seen. The Tree of Life was not just a distant promise but a present reality, made accessible through faith in the Messiah.

He gathered the faithful and spoke of the vision, his voice trembling with both reverence and joy.

"The Tree of Life is more than a symbol," Peter proclaimed. "It is the assurance of eternal communion with God. In Christ, the way is opened, and the promise is fulfilled. Let us live as those who are destined to partake of its fruit."

Peter's words stirred a deep longing in his listeners. Some wept with the realization of what had been lost in Eden but rejoiced at the hope of restoration. Others knelt in prayer, committing themselves to the path of faith that led to the tree.

Through his testimony, Peter emphasized the centrality of the Tree of Life to the divine plan. It was not just a reminder of humanity's fall but a beacon of hope, pointing to the redemption and restoration promised by the Creator.

And as Peter continued to proclaim the vision, he prayed that all who heard would embrace the invitation to eternal life, finding in the Tree of Life the fulfillment of every longing and the promise of a love that never ends.

Chapter 16
The River of Life

The vision unfolded with a brilliance that seemed to flow like liquid light, cascading through Peter's senses and drawing him into the heart of the New Jerusalem. There, at the throne of God and the Lamb, he saw a river unlike any he had ever known. It shimmered with a crystalline purity, its waters alive with a radiance that defied earthly comparison.

"This is the River of Life," the voice said, gentle yet resounding. "It flows from my throne, carrying the essence of my Spirit to all who dwell in my presence."

Peter stood at the river's edge, overwhelmed by its beauty. The waters moved with a serene power, their surface reflecting the light of eternity. Yet this was no ordinary river. It was the source of renewal, healing, and unending vitality. Its current whispered of creation's restoration, of every tear wiped away, and every sorrow turned to joy.

The banks of the river were adorned with the Tree of Life, its roots nourished by the living waters. The tree bore fruit in every season, its abundance a testimony to the unceasing provision of the Creator. The leaves of the tree shimmered like emeralds, their touch promising healing for the nations.

The vision shifted, and Peter was transported to the beginning of creation. He saw the rivers that flowed from Eden, dividing into streams that nourished the earth. These rivers carried the original blessing of life, spreading abundance and fertility to all corners of the garden.

Yet as the vision unfolded, Peter witnessed the devastating consequences of humanity's fall. The rivers grew dark, their purity tainted by sin. What was meant to bring life became a witness to death and corruption.

The voice spoke, heavy with both judgment and hope. "The waters were defiled, but they will flow pure once more. My covenant is everlasting, and I will restore what has been lost."

Peter was then carried forward through the Scriptures, seeing glimpses of the River of Life's promise echoed in the words of the prophets. Ezekiel's vision of a temple from which waters flowed, bringing life to the desert and healing to the Dead Sea, came alive before Peter's eyes. The river widened as it flowed, its depth increasing with every step.

"Wherever the river goes," the voice declared, "there will be life. The barren places will be renewed, and the desolate lands will bloom."

Peter marveled at the hope embedded in these images—a promise that the Creator's Spirit would one day flow freely, restoring all that had been broken.

The vision shifted again, and Peter stood beside the Messiah as He spoke to a crowd. The words resonated with power and simplicity: "If anyone thirsts, let him come to me and drink. Whoever believes in me, as the Scripture has said, 'Out of his heart will flow rivers of living water.'"

Peter now understood that the River of Life was not merely a future promise but a present reality, made accessible through the Messiah. The living water, a symbol of the Spirit, was poured out to quench the deepest thirst of humanity's soul.

He saw the woman at the well, her face etched with weariness and shame, transformed as the Messiah offered her the gift of living water. "Everyone who drinks this water will be thirsty again," He said, "but whoever drinks the water I give him will never thirst."

Peter's heart swelled as the vision returned to the New Jerusalem, where the River of Life flowed freely, its waters bringing joy to every corner of the city. There were no barriers, no boundaries; all who had overcome were welcome to partake.

"This is my promise to my people," the voice said. "No longer will there be thirst, for the river flows eternally. In it is life, and that life is the light of all who dwell with me."

Peter saw people from every nation, tribe, and tongue gathered along the riverbanks. They knelt to drink, their faces alight with joy and peace. The waters did more than quench thirst—they healed wounds, washed away sorrows, and restored the weary to strength.

The vision lingered, revealing the inexhaustible nature of the river. Unlike earthly streams that ebb and flow, the River of Life was eternal, its source the Creator Himself. It carried with it the fullness of divine love, grace, and renewal.

Peter felt the river's flow within his own spirit, a foretaste of the promise that would one day be fulfilled for all who believed. It was a reminder that the Creator's provision was not bound by time or circumstance but was always sufficient.

When Peter returned from the vision, his soul was refreshed and invigorated. He spoke to the faithful, his words flowing like the river he had seen.

"The River of Life is not just a promise for the future," Peter declared. "It flows now through the Spirit of God, bringing renewal and hope to all who thirst. Come and drink deeply, for the waters are freely given."

Peter's testimony stirred a deep longing among his listeners. Some wept as they realized the emptiness of their lives apart from the living water. Others rejoiced, their spirits renewed by the assurance of the river's eternal flow.

Through his words, Peter emphasized the centrality of the River of Life to the divine plan. It was a symbol of restoration, an invitation to intimacy with the Creator, and a foretaste of the eternal joy that awaited those who believed.

And as Peter continued to proclaim the vision, he prayed that all who heard would come to the river, finding in its waters the life, healing, and joy that flowed from the heart of the Creator Himself.

Chapter 17
The Gates of Paradise

The vision opened with an awe-inspiring sight: a city descending from the heavens, its brilliance eclipsing even the sun. This was the New Jerusalem, the eternal dwelling place of the righteous, whose foundations were adorned with every precious stone and whose streets shimmered like gold refined to glass. At the heart of this celestial city stood the Gates of Paradise, twelve in number, each fashioned from a single pearl, their grandeur defying mortal comprehension.

"These are the gates," the voice declared, its resonance imbued with majesty and welcome. "Through them, my people enter into everlasting communion with me."

Peter approached the gates, his spirit trembling with both reverence and joy. Each gate bore the name of one of the twelve tribes of Israel, a testament to the fulfillment of the covenant made with Abraham. Standing before the gates, Peter felt a sense of completion—as though all of history had led to this moment, where creation was reconciled with its Creator.

The gates were open wide, their luminous surfaces reflecting the glory of the city within. Yet Peter noticed something unusual: no guards, no locks, no barriers. The gates stood perpetually open, their invitation eternal and unchanging.

"Here," the voice explained, "there is no night, no fear, and no enemy to close the gates against. Only the righteous may enter, for their names are written in the Lamb's Book of Life."

The vision shifted, and Peter was transported to the time of the earthly tabernacle and temple. He saw the gates of the sanctuary, symbols of God's presence among His people, yet marked by separation. Only the priests could pass through the outer gates, and only the high priest could enter the innermost place.

Peter was reminded of the cherubim who had guarded the gates of Eden, barring humanity from the Tree of Life. Those gates, once a symbol of exclusion, had now been transformed into an eternal invitation.

"The gates of Paradise," the voice said, "are open because of the sacrifice of my Son. Through Him, what was lost in Eden is restored."

Peter's spirit was drawn closer to the gates, and he saw the multitudes entering. These were the redeemed, clothed in garments of light, their faces radiant with joy. Men and women from every nation, tribe, and tongue passed through, their voices lifting in songs of praise.

"No one enters by their own merit," the voice said. "The Lamb has paid the price, and through His blood, they are made worthy."

Peter marveled at the unity of those entering the city. There was no division, no strife—only a shared recognition of the grace that had brought them to this place.

The vision expanded, revealing the paths that led to the gates. Peter saw the trials and triumphs of those who journeyed toward them. Some walked through deserts of despair, others climbed mountains of sacrifice, and still others crossed valleys of tears. Yet all were sustained by the hope of reaching the city.

At each gate, Peter saw angels, not as guards but as greeters. Their presence was a reminder of the heavenly joy that accompanied each soul's arrival. As one weary traveler approached, an angel spoke, "Enter into the joy of your Lord, for your faith has brought you home."

The voice then revealed a sobering truth. "Not all will enter these gates. Many have turned away, rejecting the invitation of my Son. They chose the wide road that leads to destruction, though my call was to the narrow path that leads to life."

Peter was shown those who stood outside the city, their faces marked by regret and longing. The gates, though open, were inaccessible to them, for they had refused the grace that made entry possible.

Tears filled Peter's eyes as he witnessed the separation. Yet even here, the voice offered hope. "The gates remain open, as does my mercy. Until the end, all who repent may yet enter."

The vision returned to the brilliance of the city, where Peter saw the fulfillment of every promise. Within the gates, there was no more pain, no more death, and no more sorrow. The inhabitants of the city walked in the light of the Lamb, their joy complete.

The gates themselves seemed to radiate the love of the Creator, standing as eternal reminders of His faithfulness and His desire to dwell with His people.

"These gates," the voice said, "are the fulfillment of my covenant. Through them, my children come home, and my dwelling place is with them forever."

When Peter returned from the vision, his heart overflowed with both joy and urgency. The gates of Paradise were more than a symbol—they were the ultimate destination for all who believed, the culmination of the journey of faith.

He gathered the faithful and shared the vision, his voice filled with hope and conviction.

"The gates of Paradise are open," Peter proclaimed. "Through Christ, we are invited to enter and dwell in the presence of God forever. Let us not delay but walk the path that leads to life, for the invitation is for all who will receive it."

Peter's testimony stirred his listeners deeply. Some resolved to renew their faith, committing themselves to the path that led to the gates. Others, burdened by the weight of their sin, found hope in the assurance that the gates remained open to the repentant.

Through his words, Peter emphasized the centrality of the gates to the divine plan. They were not just a point of entry but a promise of eternal communion with the Creator.

And as Peter continued to proclaim the vision, he prayed that all who heard would set their eyes on the Gates of Paradise, walking the narrow path that led to the city of light and the everlasting embrace of their Creator.

Chapter 18
The Eternal Fire

The vision enveloped Peter in a realm of profound intensity, where light and heat radiated from an unquenchable source. Before him roared the Eternal Fire, a presence both magnificent and terrifying. It was no ordinary flame, for it burned with purpose and judgment, illuminating the divine nature of justice and purification.

"This is the Eternal Fire," the voice said, its tone heavy with both sorrow and resolve. "It is the fire of my holiness, the instrument of my judgment, and the means of refining all creation."

Peter stood at the edge of the fire, feeling its searing heat yet untouched by its flames. The fire was alive, its movements deliberate, consuming all that was impure while preserving what was righteous. Peter realized that this was not a fire of random destruction but of perfect intent—a reflection of the Creator's justice.

He saw within the flames the residue of sin and rebellion, reduced to ash and swept away. Yet he also saw the fire purifying what was good, burning away dross to reveal the beauty and purity of the Creator's work.

"This fire is not for destruction alone," the voice explained, "but for renewal. Through it, I restore what sin has marred and refine what I have created."

The vision shifted, and Peter was transported to moments in Scripture where fire symbolized the presence of the Almighty. He stood with Moses before the burning bush, a flame that burned without consuming, signifying the holiness of God.

He witnessed the fire that descended on Mount Sinai, where the people trembled at the display of divine majesty. He saw the pillar of fire that led the Israelites through the wilderness, a sign of the Creator's guidance and protection.

"Fire is my presence," the voice said. "It is both a light to guide and a force to purify."

Peter's spirit was drawn to another scene: the tongues of fire that descended upon the apostles at Pentecost. These flames did not destroy but empowered, filling the disciples with the Holy Spirit and igniting their mission to spread the Gospel.

"This fire brings life," the voice declared. "It cleanses, renews, and equips my people for the work of my kingdom."

Peter now understood that the Eternal Fire was not confined to judgment alone but was also a source of transformation. It was a fire that consumed sin but preserved and empowered the faithful.

The vision grew darker as Peter was shown the fire of judgment, reserved for those who had rejected the Creator's grace. He saw the unrepentant cast into a lake of fire, their rebellion finally meeting the justice it had long denied.

Peter recoiled at the sight, his heart aching for those who suffered. Yet he felt the weight of the truth—that the fire was not an act of cruelty but of righteousness.

"The fire reveals the choices of each soul," the voice said. "It is a refining fire for the faithful and a consuming fire for the wicked. None may escape its truth."

Peter then saw a river of fire flowing from the throne of God, consuming all that was unholy and leaving a renewed creation in its wake. The heavens and the earth were made new, cleansed of sin and death, their beauty restored to its original glory.

"This is the final work of the fire," the voice declared. "It brings forth a new heaven and a new earth, where righteousness dwells, and my people live in peace forever."

As the vision faded, Peter returned to the world with a deep understanding of the Eternal Fire's dual nature. It was both a force of judgment and a promise of renewal, a manifestation of the Creator's justice and love.

He gathered the faithful and shared the vision, his voice steady yet filled with urgency.

"The Eternal Fire is not to be feared by those who walk in righteousness," Peter said. "It is the fire of God's holiness, refining us and making us new. Yet it is also a fire of judgment, revealing the truth of every heart. Let us live as those who seek the light, purified by His love."

Peter's words stirred a profound response among his listeners. Some wept, recognizing the need to turn from sin and embrace the refining power of God's Spirit. Others found comfort in the promise of renewal, knowing that the fire would bring forth the beauty of God's creation.

Through his testimony, Peter emphasized the Eternal Fire as a central aspect of the divine plan. It was not a threat but a promise—a force that revealed the truth, purified the faithful, and renewed all things.

And as Peter continued to proclaim the vision, he prayed that all who heard would submit to the refining fire of the Creator, finding in it the path to holiness and the promise of eternal peace.

Chapter 19
The Outer Darkness

The vision drew Peter into a realm unlike any he had encountered before. It was vast and unending, a void where light did not shine, and the air itself seemed heavy with despair. This was the Outer Darkness, a place of separation and sorrow, where those who had turned away from the Creator dwelt apart from His presence.

"This is the place reserved for those who chose the path of rebellion," the voice said, resonating with both sorrow and justice. "Here, they are separated from the light of my face, for they rejected the life I offered."

Peter stood at the edge of this abyss, his heart trembling as he beheld its bleakness. The darkness was not merely an absence of light but a tangible force, oppressive and suffocating. Within it, Peter could hear faint echoes—cries of anguish, whispers of regret, and the mournful lament of souls who had chosen to walk away from the love of their Creator.

"This is the consequence of their choice," the voice continued. "I offered them life, yet they turned to death. I called them to my light, yet they embraced the shadows."

The vision shifted, showing Peter glimpses of those who had found themselves in the Outer Darkness. He saw the proud, who had built their lives on their own achievements and rejected the humility required to seek the Creator. He saw the cruel, whose hearts had hardened against the cries of the needy and the oppressed. He saw the indifferent, those who had turned a blind eye to truth and love, consumed by their own desires.

Each soul was burdened by the weight of their choices, their separation from the Creator a source of endless torment. Yet

Peter noticed that their suffering was not inflicted but self-contained, the natural result of rejecting the only source of life and light.

"Their torment is not my doing," the voice explained. "It is the consequence of a life lived apart from me. The darkness reflects the void within their hearts, a void that only my presence could have filled."

Peter was shown the gates that led to the Outer Darkness. These gates, unlike the gates of Paradise, were closed—not by divine decree but by the choice of those within. He saw the faint outlines of figures approaching the gates, longing to escape, yet unable to relinquish the pride, anger, or despair that held them captive.

"They are bound by their own chains," the voice said. "For repentance requires surrender, and they cannot bear to yield."

Peter's heart ached as he realized that the Outer Darkness was not a prison imposed by the Creator but the ultimate expression of human freedom—the freedom to reject the light and choose the shadows.

The vision turned to those who had escaped the darkness, their faces filled with a newfound peace. Peter saw how repentance, even in the depths of despair, could break the chains that bound them. These souls, though scarred by their journey, were welcomed into the light, their burdens lifted by the grace of the Creator.

"My mercy reaches even here," the voice said, filled with compassion. "For those who turn to me, the gates will open, and the light will welcome them home."

Peter then saw the connection between the Outer Darkness and the choices made in life. He was shown scenes of people who had ignored the call of the Spirit, their hearts growing colder with each rejection. He saw how small decisions—acts of selfishness, cruelty, or indifference—accumulated into a life turned away from the Creator.

Yet he also saw moments where the Spirit intervened, offering opportunities for repentance and renewal. Some responded, their lives transformed by grace. Others turned away, their hearts hardened further by their refusal.

"The darkness is not inevitable," the voice said. "Every soul is given the chance to choose the light. My call is unceasing, and my mercy endures, but the choice remains theirs."

The vision returned to the present, and Peter stood once more at the edge of the Outer Darkness. He felt the weight of the revelation, understanding that this place was not just a consequence but a warning—a reminder of the cost of turning away from the Creator's love.

When Peter returned from the vision, he gathered the faithful, his heart heavy yet filled with resolve.

"The Outer Darkness is real," he said, his voice trembling with urgency. "It is a place of separation, where the absence of God's light becomes a torment of its own. Yet it is not the end for those who turn to Him. His mercy reaches even the deepest shadows."

Peter's testimony struck his listeners deeply. Some wept as they reflected on the state of their own hearts, recognizing the need to turn from the shadows and embrace the light. Others found hope in the assurance that no soul was beyond the reach of the Creator's grace.

Through his words, Peter emphasized the importance of living in the light, making choices that reflected the love and truth of the Creator. The Outer Darkness was not a punishment to be feared but a warning to be heeded, a call to walk in the light before it was too late.

And as Peter continued to proclaim the vision, he prayed that all who heard would reject the shadows, embracing the light of the Creator and the eternal joy of His presence.

Chapter 20
The Demons

The vision carried Peter into a realm of shadow, where the air itself seemed alive with malice. He found himself on the threshold of a great abyss, its depths teeming with restless movement. Figures darted within the darkness, their forms twisted and grotesque, their presence radiating an aura of unrelenting hatred. These were the demons—the fallen servants of the Adversary, the ancient foes of humanity.

"These," the voice said, filled with both sorrow and unyielding authority, "are the rebellious ones, cast from my presence. They seek to destroy, to deceive, and to enslave, for their hearts are bound to the darkness they chose."

Peter's gaze was drawn to the demons' forms. Once radiant beings created to serve the Almighty, they now bore the scars of their rebellion. Their beauty had been marred by their defiance, their wings stripped of glory, their light extinguished by their choice to follow Lucifer.

Peter saw their ceaseless activity, a frenzy driven by hatred for the Creator and envy of humanity. They moved through the shadows, their whispers weaving lies and sowing discord among the children of men.

"They cannot create," the voice said, "only corrupt. They cannot love, only destroy. Yet their power is not absolute, for I am the sovereign Lord, and their time is limited."

The vision shifted, showing Peter the origin of these beings. He was taken back to the rebellion in heaven, where Lucifer, the most radiant of the angels, led a third of the heavenly host in defiance against the Creator. Peter saw the battle that ensued, where Michael and the faithful angels stood firm, casting the rebels out of heaven.

The fallen angels were consigned to the abyss, their defeat complete. Yet their hatred endured, and their wrath turned toward humanity, the image-bearers of the Creator.

"They seek to mar my creation," the voice explained. "Through lies, they lead the hearts of men astray, and through fear, they enslave. Yet they cannot overcome the light, for my truth remains eternal."

Peter was then shown how demons operated within the world. He saw their subtle influence in whispers of temptation, their cunning in crafting idols that drew humanity away from the Creator. He saw how they twisted the desires of the human heart, magnifying pride, greed, and lust until they consumed the soul.

Yet Peter also saw the power of faith. He witnessed moments where the name of the Messiah was invoked, and the demons recoiled, unable to withstand the authority of the one who had defeated them at the cross.

"They tremble at the name of my Son," the voice said. "For He has triumphed over them, disarming their power and declaring their ultimate defeat."

The vision grew darker as Peter was shown the torments demons inflicted upon those who had given themselves over to darkness. He saw souls bound in chains of their own making, tormented by the very desires they had once embraced. Yet even here, Peter saw the flicker of hope.

The voice spoke again. "My mercy extends even to the tormented. Though the demons seek to hold them, they cannot stand against repentance and the power of my Spirit."

Peter witnessed moments of deliverance, where the chains of darkness were broken, and souls were freed by the light of the Creator. The demons fled, their hold shattered by the faith and prayers of the righteous.

Peter's spirit was drawn back to the present, and he saw the battle that continued around him. It was not a battle of flesh and blood but of principalities and powers, a spiritual war fought in the hearts of humanity.

The voice offered both warning and reassurance. "Be vigilant, for the enemy prowls like a roaring lion, seeking whom he may devour. Yet fear not, for I am with you. Put on the armor of faith, and stand firm in the light."

The vision concluded with a glimpse of the demons' ultimate fate. Peter saw them cast into the lake of fire, their rebellion finally meeting its end. Their power extinguished, their lies silenced, and their torment eternal, they would no longer trouble the people of God.

"Their defeat is assured," the voice declared. "For my Son has triumphed, and the day of their destruction draws near."

When Peter returned from the vision, his heart was filled with a mixture of sorrow and determination. The reality of the demons' presence and their relentless pursuit of humanity was a sobering truth. Yet the power of the Messiah and the promise of their ultimate defeat gave him strength.

He gathered the faithful and spoke of the vision, his voice both grave and resolute.

"The demons seek to lead us astray," Peter warned. "They are cunning and relentless, but they are not invincible. In Christ, we have victory. Let us resist their lies, stand firm in the truth, and cling to the light."

Peter's words stirred his listeners to vigilance. Some confessed their struggles, seeking deliverance from the chains of temptation. Others prayed fervently, asking for strength to resist the enemy's schemes.

Through his testimony, Peter emphasized the need for spiritual awareness and the power of faith. The demons were real, but so was the victory of the Messiah.

And as Peter continued to proclaim the vision, he prayed that all who heard would stand firm in the light, protected by the armor of faith, and guided by the truth of the Creator.

Chapter 21
The Antichrist

The vision opened with a chilling stillness, drawing Peter into a realm where shadows loomed large, and the air itself seemed heavy with deception. At the center of this vision stood a figure of great power and charisma, commanding the attention and adoration of countless multitudes. This was the Antichrist, the great deceiver foretold to oppose Christ and lead many astray.

"This is the one who comes in my Son's name, yet stands against Him," the voice said, its tone filled with both sorrow and unyielding authority. "He is the culmination of all rebellion, the embodiment of deceit, and the adversary of truth."

Peter's gaze was drawn to the Antichrist, whose appearance was both captivating and unsettling. The figure exuded a magnetic charm, his words dripping with persuasive eloquence. Nations rallied to him, their leaders pledging loyalty, their peoples offering worship. He promised peace and prosperity, yet beneath his veneer of benevolence lay the seeds of chaos and destruction.

Peter observed as the Antichrist performed signs and wonders, his power mesmerizing the masses. The blind saw, the lame walked, and the desperate found false hope in his touch. Yet these miracles, far from being acts of grace, were deceptions designed to mimic the works of Christ and lead hearts away from the Creator.

"The Antichrist's power is not his own," the voice explained. "It is given to him by the Adversary, whose lies fuel his rise. Yet his reign is fleeting, for truth cannot be overcome by falsehood."

The vision shifted, and Peter saw the Antichrist seated on a throne of earthly splendor. His rule extended across the globe, uniting nations under his banner. Yet this unity was not born of righteousness but of coercion and fear. Those who refused to bow were persecuted, their loyalty to the true King making them enemies of the state.

Peter's heart ached as he witnessed the suffering of the faithful. They were mocked, imprisoned, and executed, their cries of pain mingling with prayers of steadfast faith. Yet even in their suffering, their testimony shone brightly, a beacon of hope in a world overshadowed by darkness.

"They overcome by the blood of the Lamb and the word of their testimony," the voice said. "Though the Antichrist wields great power, he cannot extinguish the light of those who belong to me."

Peter was shown the subtlety of the Antichrist's deception. He did not arrive with open hostility but cloaked himself in the guise of righteousness. He spoke of unity and justice, offering solutions to humanity's deepest struggles. Yet his promises were hollow, his actions driven by a desire to supplant the Creator and exalt himself as god.

Peter saw the Antichrist desecrate holy places, setting himself up as an object of worship. Those who followed him bore his mark, a symbol of allegiance that marked their rejection of the true King.

"This is the abomination of desolation," the voice said. "It is the pinnacle of rebellion, a defiance of my holiness and a challenge to my sovereignty. Yet it shall not stand."

The vision shifted to the spiritual battle that raged behind the scenes. Peter saw angels and demons clashing in fierce combat, the heavens trembling with the force of their struggle. The Antichrist was not acting alone but was a pawn in a larger war, a battle between light and darkness that had begun long before humanity's fall.

"The Antichrist is but a shadow," the voice said, "a fleeting manifestation of rebellion. My Son's victory is eternal, and the end of this deception is assured."

Peter's gaze was drawn to the culmination of the Antichrist's reign. He saw the figure standing defiantly, rallying his followers for a final confrontation with the Lamb. The earth itself seemed to hold its breath as the armies of darkness gathered, their strength seemingly insurmountable.

But then, with a word, the Lamb appeared. His radiance eclipsed the darkness, and His authority was absolute. The Antichrist and his followers were cast down, their rebellion ended in an instant. The heavens rejoiced, and the faithful lifted their voices in triumph, proclaiming the eternal reign of the true King.

When Peter returned from the vision, his spirit burned with both urgency and hope. The Antichrist was a figure of great power and deception, yet his reign was destined to fall before the glory of the Messiah.

Peter gathered the faithful and spoke of the vision, his voice filled with conviction.

"The Antichrist will come," Peter declared. "He will deceive many, offering promises that lead to destruction. But fear not, for his power is fleeting, and his end is certain. Stand firm in the truth, for the Lamb has overcome, and His victory is eternal."

Peter's words inspired both vigilance and courage among his listeners. Some committed themselves anew to the truth, resolving to resist the lies of the enemy. Others found hope in the assurance that the Messiah's victory was already secured.

Through his testimony, Peter emphasized the need for discernment and faithfulness. The Antichrist's reign was a time of trial, but it was also an opportunity for the faithful to shine as lights in the darkness.

And as Peter continued to proclaim the vision, he prayed that all who heard would stand firm in their faith, resisting the deception of the Antichrist and holding fast to the eternal hope found in the true King.

Chapter 22
The Beast of the Apocalypse

The vision unfolded with an ominous intensity, transporting Peter to a vast, turbulent sea. From its depths rose a monstrous figure, its form grotesque and fearsome, crowned with blasphemous names. This was the Beast of the Apocalypse, a symbol of evil power and a force of chaos unleashed upon the world.

"This is the Beast," the voice said, resonating with sorrow and righteous anger. "It is the manifestation of rebellion, empowered by the Adversary to persecute my people and deceive the nations."

Peter's eyes widened as he beheld the Beast in its full form. It had ten horns and seven heads, each horn crowned with a diadem, a mockery of divine authority. Its body was a grotesque amalgamation of animals, symbolizing its ferocity and cunning. The Beast moved with a terrifying majesty, its presence darkening the world around it.

The sea from which it emerged roiled with turmoil, symbolizing the chaos and unrest of nations. Peter understood that the Beast was not just an individual but a system of power and oppression—a union of corrupt forces that opposed the Creator and sought to dominate humanity.

"The Beast arises where rebellion flourishes," the voice explained. "It draws its strength from the Adversary, yet its power is allowed only for a time."

The vision shifted, showing the Beast's rise to dominion. Peter saw it gain the allegiance of kings and nations, its authority accepted without question. It spoke with arrogance, blaspheming the Creator and demanding worship. Those who refused were cast out, their lives marked by suffering and persecution.

Peter's heart ached as he witnessed the suffering of the faithful. Yet amid their trials, he saw their unwavering resolve. Though they were rejected by the world, they held fast to the name of the Lamb, their allegiance to the true King unshaken.

"They overcome by their faith," the voice said, "for the Beast cannot touch their souls. Their names are written in the Book of Life, and they shall reign with me forever."

The vision expanded, revealing the spiritual significance of the Beast's actions. It was a tool of the Adversary, designed to counterfeit the kingdom of God and lead humanity astray. Peter saw how it wielded deception, offering false hope and promises of prosperity.

"The Beast seeks to imitate my Son," the voice explained. "Its words seem wise, its actions seem just, but its heart is filled with lies. It is the great deceiver, leading many to destruction."

Peter was shown how the Beast worked in tandem with a second figure, the False Prophet, who performed signs and wonders to validate the Beast's authority. Together, they created a counterfeit trinity, a perversion of divine truth designed to enslave humanity.

The vision turned darker as Peter saw the mark of the Beast—a symbol of allegiance imprinted on the foreheads or hands of its followers. Those who bore the mark were allowed to buy and sell, their lives seemingly secure under the Beast's dominion.

But Peter saw the true cost of the mark. It was not merely a physical sign but a spiritual commitment, a rejection of the Creator and an acceptance of the Beast's lies. The mark brought temporary comfort but eternal separation from the light of God.

"Those who take the mark," the voice said, "choose the path of destruction. Yet even here, my mercy is present. Until the end, I call them to repentance."

Peter's spirit was lifted as the vision revealed the Beast's downfall. He saw the Lamb descend in glory, His presence overwhelming the darkness. The Beast and the False Prophet were captured and cast into the lake of fire, their dominion ended in a moment.

The faithful, once oppressed, now stood victorious, their robes washed white in the blood of the Lamb. They lifted their voices in songs of triumph, declaring the eternal reign of the true King.

"The Beast's power is temporary," the voice declared. "My Son's kingdom is eternal. The faithful shall inherit the earth, and the wicked shall be no more."

When Peter returned from the vision, his heart burned with both urgency and hope. The Beast of the Apocalypse was a fearsome foe, yet its defeat was assured by the victory of the Messiah.

He gathered the faithful and spoke of the vision, his voice steady with conviction.

"The Beast will rise," Peter proclaimed. "It will deceive many and persecute the faithful, but do not fear. Its power is limited, and its end is certain. Hold fast to the Lamb, for in Him we find our victory."

Peter's words stirred his listeners to vigilance and faith. Some wept as they resolved to resist the lies of the Beast, committing themselves anew to the truth of the Messiah. Others prayed for strength, knowing that the trials ahead would test their resolve.

Through his testimony, Peter emphasized the need for discernment and courage. The Beast's reign was a time of testing, but it was also an opportunity for the faithful to shine as lights in the darkness.

And as Peter continued to proclaim the vision, he prayed that all who heard would stand firm in their faith, resisting the deception of the Beast and holding fast to the eternal hope found in the Lamb.

Chapter 23
The Number of the Beast

The vision opened with an air of unease, as Peter stood before a vast, tumultuous crowd. The people moved as though bound by a single will, their foreheads and hands marked with an ominous symbol. Above them loomed the figure of the Beast, its presence oppressive and all-encompassing.

"This is the mark of allegiance," the voice declared, its tone grave and unyielding. "It is the symbol of those who reject my truth and embrace the dominion of the Beast."

Peter's gaze was drawn to the mark—a number both simple and profound: **666**.

"This is the Number of the Beast," the voice continued. "It is the mark of humanity's rebellion and the culmination of deceit. Let him who has wisdom calculate its meaning."

Peter was shown how the mark spread across the world, enforced by the Beast and the False Prophet. Those who accepted it gained access to the marketplaces, to commerce and prosperity. They seemed to thrive, their lives untouched by the suffering inflicted on those who refused. Yet Peter saw the deeper truth beneath the surface.

The mark was not just a tool of economic control but a sign of spiritual submission. Those who bore it had willingly chosen to align themselves with the Beast, rejecting the Creator's sovereignty. The mark symbolized their allegiance to a false kingdom, one built on lies and destined for destruction.

"The mark is more than a number," the voice explained. "It is a declaration of the heart—a choice to follow the path of rebellion rather than the way of life."

The vision shifted, showing Peter the plight of those who refused the mark. They were cast out from society, unable to buy or sell, their lives marked by hardship and persecution. Yet their faces shone with a light that could not be extinguished, their faith in the Lamb sustaining them through every trial.

"They are my faithful ones," the voice said, filled with love and pride. "Though the world rejects them, they are mine, and I will never forsake them."

Peter saw the strength of their conviction as they resisted the pressure to conform. They endured ridicule, imprisonment, and even death, yet they clung to the promise of eternal life.

"The mark of the Beast is temporary," the voice said, "but my seal is eternal. Those who are marked by my Spirit will reign with me forever."

Peter's understanding deepened as he was shown the meaning behind the number 666. It was the number of man, a representation of humanity's attempt to exalt itself above the Creator. The repetition of six, falling short of the divine perfection symbolized by seven, was a reminder of humanity's imperfection and rebellion.

"This is the counterfeit of my kingdom," the voice said. "The Beast seeks to imitate my authority, yet it can never attain the completeness of my will."

Peter saw how the number became a rallying cry for those who sought power and control apart from the Creator. It was a symbol of arrogance, a declaration of independence from the divine order.

The vision turned to the ultimate fate of those who bore the mark. Peter saw them gathered before the throne of judgment, their allegiance to the Beast laid bare. They were cast into the lake of fire, their choice to reject the Creator sealing their destiny.

Yet even here, Peter felt the sorrow of the Creator, whose love had been extended to them time and again.

"My desire is that none should perish," the voice said, heavy with lament. "But they have chosen the path of destruction, and I honor their choice."

Peter's spirit was lifted as the vision returned to the faithful, those who had refused the mark and remained steadfast. He saw them clothed in white robes, their names written in the Lamb's Book of Life. They stood before the throne, their faces radiant with joy, their trials forgotten in the glory of the eternal kingdom.

"These are my overcomers," the voice declared. "They have rejected the mark of the Beast and embraced the seal of my Spirit. To them belongs the crown of life."

When Peter returned from the vision, his heart burned with both urgency and hope. The Number of the Beast was more than a symbol; it was a choice that humanity would face—a decision between allegiance to the Creator and submission to the lies of the Adversary.

He gathered the faithful and spoke of the vision, his voice steady yet filled with passion.

"The mark of the Beast is a deception," Peter warned. "It promises comfort but leads to destruction. Resist it with all your strength, for the seal of the Lamb is your true protection. In Him, you will find life everlasting."

Peter's testimony stirred his listeners to vigilance. Some resolved to deepen their faith, preparing their hearts to stand firm in the face of temptation. Others wept as they sought forgiveness, renouncing the ways in which they had strayed.

Through his words, Peter emphasized the importance of discernment and faithfulness. The Number of the Beast was not to be feared but to be understood, a reminder of the spiritual battle that raged around them.

And as Peter continued to proclaim the vision, he prayed that all who heard would reject the lies of the Beast, standing firm in the truth of the Creator and bearing the seal of the Lamb, a mark of eternal life and unshakable hope.

Chapter 24
The Great Tribulation

The vision opened with a sky thick with foreboding. The air carried a tangible weight, as though creation itself held its breath. Peter was drawn into a world plunged into chaos and suffering—a time unlike any other in the history of humanity. This was the Great Tribulation, a period of unparalleled distress and testing that would precede the culmination of the Creator's divine plan.

"This is the time of trial," the voice said, solemn and unyielding. "It is a refining fire for the faithful and a final call to repentance for the wayward."

Peter's gaze was drawn to the earth below, where nations and kingdoms convulsed in turmoil. Wars erupted on every horizon, their fires consuming cities and fields alike. Famine swept across the lands, its merciless grip sparing neither the mighty nor the lowly. Pestilence followed in its wake, a silent yet relentless destroyer.

Amid this chaos, the earth itself seemed to revolt. Peter saw earthquakes that tore through mountains, tsunamis that swallowed coastlines, and storms of such ferocity that even the heavens trembled. The elements, once bound in order, now unleashed their full power, reflecting the unraveling of humanity's own heart.

"These are the birth pains," the voice explained. "They herald the coming of my kingdom, yet they are not the end. In the midst of this suffering, my mercy remains."

The vision turned to the faithful, those who bore the name of the Lamb. Peter saw them scattered across the earth, their lives marked by suffering and persecution. They were hunted by the

Beast, ostracized for refusing its mark, and subjected to trials that tested the depths of their faith.

Yet Peter also saw their resilience. Their prayers rose like incense, their songs of praise defiant against the darkness. Though their bodies were broken, their spirits burned brightly, a testimony to the hope that sustained them.

"They are my witnesses," the voice said, filled with love and pride. "Through their endurance, they proclaim my truth to a world on the brink of destruction."

Peter's spirit was then drawn to those who had turned their backs on the Creator. He saw them overwhelmed by fear and despair, their hearts hardened by pride and rebellion. Some sought refuge in the promises of the Beast, clinging to its false assurances of security. Others cursed the heavens, their anger a futile rebellion against the Creator's authority.

Yet even among these, Peter saw glimmers of repentance. A few, broken by the weight of their choices, fell to their knees and cried out for mercy. The Creator's response was swift and unwavering, His grace extended to all who turned to Him.

"My mercy endures," the voice said, its tone both tender and firm. "Even in the midst of judgment, I call to them. Let the one who thirsts come and drink freely from the water of life."

The vision shifted to the spiritual realm, where Peter saw the forces of light and darkness locked in battle. Angels, radiant and resolute, clashed with the demonic hosts of the Adversary. The heavens trembled with the fury of their struggle, yet Peter sensed the unwavering authority of the Creator presiding over it all.

"This is not a war of equals," the voice declared. "The victory is mine, and it has already been won through my Son. This battle is but the fulfillment of my justice and the revelation of my glory."

Peter was shown the perseverance of the faithful during the Tribulation. They gathered in secret, their fellowship a source of strength and encouragement. They shared what little they had, their acts of kindness and sacrifice reflecting the love of the Lamb.

Despite the overwhelming darkness, Peter saw how their testimony brought others to faith. The light of their witness pierced the shadows, drawing those who were lost into the fold of the Creator's mercy.

"They are the salt of the earth," the voice said. "Through their suffering, my truth is revealed, and my kingdom advances."

As the vision reached its climax, Peter saw the culmination of the Great Tribulation. The heavens opened, and the Lamb appeared, clothed in glory and surrounded by the hosts of heaven. His presence was overwhelming, a light that consumed the darkness and brought all things into the fullness of His authority.

The nations trembled, their power brought low before the King of kings. The faithful were lifted up, their tears wiped away, their trials replaced with eternal joy. The Lamb's voice resounded across creation: **"Behold, I am making all things new."**

When Peter returned from the vision, his heart was heavy with the gravity of what he had seen but also alight with hope. The Great Tribulation was a time of immense suffering, yet it was also a time of unparalleled grace and renewal.

He gathered the faithful and shared the vision, his voice steady yet filled with urgency.

"The Great Tribulation will test the hearts of all," Peter proclaimed. "It will separate the faithful from the faithless, the true from the false. Yet even in the darkest hour, the light of the Lamb will shine. Stand firm, for His coming is near, and His victory is assured."

Peter's testimony stirred his listeners deeply. Some trembled at the warnings, resolving to prepare their hearts for the trials to come. Others found comfort in the assurance that the Creator's mercy would remain even in the midst of judgment.

Through his words, Peter emphasized the importance of endurance and faithfulness. The Great Tribulation was not just a time of suffering but a divine refining, a call to steadfast hope and unwavering trust in the Lamb.

And as Peter continued to proclaim the vision, he prayed that all who heard would stand firm, holding fast to the promises of the Creator, and awaiting the glorious return of the Lamb who would bring an end to the darkness and establish His eternal reign.

Chapter 25
The Rapture

The vision began with a sudden and overwhelming brightness, as though the heavens themselves were being torn open. Peter found himself gazing upward into the infinite expanse of the sky, where radiant figures appeared, their forms glowing with the glory of the Creator. The faithful, who had endured the trials of the earth, were being drawn upward, their faces alight with joy and awe.

"This is the Rapture," the voice declared, resounding with both triumph and reassurance. "It is the gathering of my people, called to meet my Son in the air, to be with Him forever."

Peter saw the earth below, where the faithful were caught up in an instant. Some were in the midst of their daily labors, others gathered in prayer and worship, but all were suddenly transformed. Their mortal bodies were replaced with incorruptible ones, their souls freed from the weight of sin and sorrow.

The scene was not one of chaos but of divine order, a moment orchestrated with perfect precision. Those who were lifted up shared one unifying trait: their faith in the Lamb and their unwavering hope in His promise of salvation.

"This is the fulfillment of my covenant," the voice said. "They are mine, sealed by my Spirit, and now they are brought to dwell with me forever."

The vision shifted to the faithful who had passed from the earth before this moment. Peter saw graves open, their occupants rising in glory. It was a resurrection of the righteous, their souls and bodies reunited in perfection. Together with those still living, they ascended toward the presence of the Messiah, where a great celebration awaited.

Peter marveled at the unity of this gathering. Men and women from every nation, tribe, and tongue were joined together, their voices lifting in a single song of praise.

"This is my church," the voice said, filled with love. "Not divided by borders or time, but united in the blood of the Lamb."

Peter's gaze was drawn to the heavenly realm, where the Raptured were brought before the throne of the Creator. The Lamb stood at the center, His wounds visible yet radiant with victory. The faithful cast their crowns before Him, their gratitude and adoration flowing like a mighty river.

Peter saw the joy on their faces, a joy that transcended any earthly understanding. It was the fulfillment of every promise, the end of every longing.

"This is their reward," the voice said. "To dwell with me, to see my face, and to share in my glory forever."

Yet the vision also revealed the earth below, now emptied of the faithful. Peter saw those who had rejected the Creator's call, their faces filled with confusion and dread. The absence of the righteous left a void that was quickly filled by fear and chaos. The forces of the Beast surged forward, their oppression unchecked.

"The Rapture is a dividing line," the voice explained. "It marks the end of mercy for those who persist in rebellion, yet it remains a testimony of my love to the world."

Peter understood that the Rapture was not only a moment of deliverance but also a final call to repentance. Those left behind were given the opportunity to turn to the Creator, though their path would now be fraught with even greater trials.

The vision shifted once more, revealing the preparation of the faithful for their eternal purpose. Peter saw them clothed in white robes, their garments reflecting the purity and righteousness of the Lamb. They were given roles in the eternal kingdom, their lives a continuation of worship and service to the Creator.

"Their journey does not end here," the voice said. "They are my beloved, and they shall reign with me in the new heaven and the new earth."

Peter's heart swelled as he witnessed the grandeur of what awaited the faithful. The Rapture was not merely an escape but a transition into the fullness of the Creator's plan—a reunion, a celebration, and the beginning of eternity.

When Peter returned from the vision, his soul was ablaze with both urgency and hope. The Rapture was not just a promise for the future but a call to live faithfully in the present, preparing hearts and minds for the moment when the Lamb would gather His own.

He gathered the faithful and shared the vision, his voice steady yet filled with passion.

"The Rapture is coming," Peter proclaimed. "It is the hope of the righteous and the fulfillment of the Lamb's promise. Be ready, for it will come in the twinkling of an eye. Live as those who belong to Him, for in Him is life eternal."

Peter's testimony stirred his listeners deeply. Some resolved to recommit their lives to the Creator, ensuring their hearts were ready for the day of the Lamb's return. Others wept with joy, their hope renewed by the assurance of their future with the Messiah.

Through his words, Peter emphasized the importance of readiness and faithfulness. The Rapture was not a moment to fear but a promise to embrace, a culmination of the Creator's love for His people.

And as Peter continued to proclaim the vision, he prayed that all who heard would live in anticipation of the Rapture, walking in faith, hope, and love until the day they were called to meet the Lamb in the air and dwell with Him forever.

Chapter 26
The Second Coming

The vision began with a sudden and overwhelming brilliance, a light that pierced through the veil of heaven and filled the earth with its glory. Peter found himself standing on a vast plain, surrounded by multitudes whose eyes turned upward in awe. The skies split open, revealing the King of kings, descending with power and majesty. This was the Second Coming of the Messiah, the moment when all creation would bow before the one who reigns forever.

"This is the fulfillment of my promise," the voice said, resonant with triumph and authority. "My Son returns to judge the nations, to vanquish evil, and to establish His eternal kingdom."

Peter's gaze was drawn to the figure of the Messiah, riding upon a white horse. His eyes were like flames of fire, His head crowned with many diadems, and His robe dipped in blood. Upon His thigh was written the name: **King of kings and Lord of lords.**

The armies of heaven followed Him, clothed in white linen, their ranks shimmering with divine radiance. They carried no weapons, for the battle would be won by the word of the Messiah alone, sharper than any sword and filled with the authority of the Creator.

Peter's heart trembled at the sight, for the Lamb who had been slain now appeared as the Lion of Judah, His presence both fearsome and magnificent.

The vision turned to the nations of the earth, gathered for the final confrontation. Peter saw the forces of the Beast amassed, their armies vast and their weapons poised for war. The rulers of the earth had united in rebellion, their pride blinding them to the futility of their cause.

Yet even as they prepared for battle, the heavens thundered, and the earth quaked. The presence of the Messiah overwhelmed them, their confidence shattered in the face of His glory.

"This is the end of rebellion," the voice declared. "The wicked shall be brought low, and the faithful shall be vindicated. My Son's justice is perfect, and His reign shall have no end."

Peter witnessed the battle, though it was unlike any earthly conflict. There were no drawn-out struggles, no clashing of swords or prolonged sieges. With a single word from the Messiah, the forces of the Beast were defeated. The Beast and the False Prophet were seized and cast into the lake of fire, their reign of terror brought to a swift and decisive end.

The multitudes who had followed them fell before the Lamb, their power undone, their rebellion silenced. The battlefield was transformed into a place of judgment, where the nations were gathered before the Messiah's throne.

The vision shifted to the judgment of the living. Peter saw the righteous separated from the wicked, as a shepherd divides the sheep from the goats. The faithful were welcomed into the eternal kingdom, their faces radiant with joy as they heard the words of the Messiah:

"Come, you who are blessed by my Father; inherit the kingdom prepared for you from the foundation of the world."

The wicked, however, were cast away, their defiance met with justice. Though their rebellion had been great, Peter sensed the sorrow in the Creator's heart.

"I take no pleasure in the death of the wicked," the voice said. "Yet justice demands that rebellion be answered, and the path they chose leads to separation from me."

Peter was then shown the transformation of the earth. The curse of sin was lifted, and creation itself was renewed. Mountains rose in splendor, rivers flowed with crystal clarity, and the skies were filled with a brilliance that reflected the glory of the Creator. The New Jerusalem descended, its gates open to all who bore the name of the Lamb.

The Messiah took His place upon the throne, His reign established in righteousness and peace. The nations brought their glory into the city, their kings bowing before the King of kings.

"This is the consummation of my plan," the voice declared. "All things are made new, and my dwelling place is with my people forever."

Peter's spirit was filled with awe as he witnessed the culmination of history. The Second Coming was not just a moment of judgment but a celebration of victory, the restoration of all that had been lost. It was the fulfillment of every promise, the answer to every prayer.

When Peter returned from the vision, his heart burned with urgency and hope. He gathered the faithful and shared what he had seen, his voice trembling with both reverence and joy.

"The King is coming," Peter proclaimed. "He will judge the nations and establish His eternal kingdom. Let us be found faithful, prepared for His return, for His justice is perfect, and His mercy endures forever."

Peter's testimony stirred his listeners deeply. Some wept with joy, their hope renewed by the promise of the Messiah's return. Others knelt in prayer, seeking to align their hearts with the will of the coming King.

Through his words, Peter emphasized the importance of readiness and faithfulness. The Second Coming was not merely a future event but a present call to live in the light of the Messiah's victory.

And as Peter continued to proclaim the vision, he prayed that all who heard would stand firm in their faith, awaiting the glorious return of the Lamb who would reign forever as the King of kings and the Lord of lords.

Chapter 27
The Millennium

The vision unfolded with a profound sense of peace and renewal. Peter stood on a transformed earth, where the scars of sin and rebellion had been healed, and creation radiated with the light of the Creator's presence. This was the beginning of the Millennium, the thousand-year reign of the Messiah, when righteousness and justice would flourish under His perfect rule.

"This is the era of my Son's dominion," the voice declared, its tone filled with majesty and joy. "In this time, my will is done on earth as it is in heaven."

Peter's gaze was drawn to the throne of the Messiah, established in the heart of the New Jerusalem. From this throne, the Lamb reigned with absolute authority, His judgments wise and His compassion unending. The nations of the earth gathered before Him, their leaders submitting to His rule, their peoples living in harmony.

The Messiah's presence was the source of light and life. There was no need for the sun or moon, for His glory illuminated all things. The River of Life flowed from the throne, its waters bringing renewal to the land, and the Tree of Life stood on its banks, bearing fruit in every season.

"This is the fulfillment of my covenant," the voice said. "Through my Son, the earth is restored, and my people dwell in peace."

Peter was shown the inhabitants of this millennial kingdom. The faithful who had endured the Great Tribulation and the Rapture now lived alongside those who had turned to the Creator in the final moments of the Tribulation. Together, they formed a community united by their devotion to the Lamb.

Peter saw children playing in fields where once there had been desolation, their laughter echoing across the land. He saw men and women working joyfully, their labors no longer tainted by toil but filled with purpose and fulfillment. The harmony extended to the animal kingdom, where predators and prey lay together in peace, a reflection of the Creator's perfect design.

"This is the restoration of Eden," the voice explained. "The curse is lifted, and my creation is as I intended it to be."

The vision turned to the spiritual reality of the Millennium. Peter saw that Satan, the great deceiver, had been bound and cast into the abyss, his power restrained for the duration of this era. Without his influence, the hearts of humanity turned toward the light, and the knowledge of the Creator filled the earth as the waters cover the sea.

Yet Peter sensed that this peace, though profound, was not the final fulfillment of the Creator's plan.

"The Adversary is bound, but his rebellion is not yet ended," the voice said. "At the appointed time, he will be released for a short season, to test the hearts of men and bring my justice to its completion."

Peter was shown the roles of the faithful during the Millennium. They reigned alongside the Messiah, their lives a reflection of His authority and grace. Some served as shepherds of communities, guiding others in righteousness. Others were stewards of creation, restoring and tending the land.

The faithful were not idle; their work was an extension of their worship, their actions a continual testimony to the glory of the Lamb.

"This is the reward of those who overcame," the voice said. "They share in my kingdom, not as servants but as co-heirs with my Son."

The vision turned to the worship of the Messiah during this era. Peter saw multitudes gather at the New Jerusalem, their voices lifting in unison to praise the King. The feasts and festivals of old took on new meaning, their rituals fulfilled in the presence of the Lamb.

Peter's heart swelled as he witnessed the joy of the people, their worship pure and untainted. The love between the Creator and His creation was fully realized, a bond unbroken and eternal.

"This is the joy of my presence," the voice said. "Here, my people know me as I know them, and they are satisfied."

As the vision neared its end, Peter was shown a glimpse of what lay beyond the Millennium. He saw the release of Satan, his deceit stirring rebellion once more among those who had not fully surrendered their hearts. Yet this final uprising was brief, its defeat absolute. The Adversary and all who followed him were cast into the lake of fire, their rebellion ended forever.

With this, the heavens and earth were made new, the eternal kingdom established in its fullness.

"This is the end of the Millennium," the voice declared, "and the beginning of eternity. My justice is complete, my mercy fulfilled, and my dwelling place with my people is forever."

When Peter returned from the vision, his heart was filled with awe and anticipation. The Millennium was not just a promise of peace but a foretaste of the eternal kingdom, a time when the reign of the Messiah would transform the earth and bring all things under His perfect authority.

He gathered the faithful and spoke of the vision, his voice steady yet filled with joy.

"The Millennium is coming," Peter proclaimed. "It is the reign of the Lamb, the restoration of all things. Let us live as those who belong to Him, preparing our hearts for the day when His justice and peace will cover the earth."

Peter's testimony stirred his listeners deeply. Some rejoiced at the promise of renewal, their hope strengthened by the assurance of the Messiah's reign. Others reflected on the responsibility of living faithfully, knowing that their lives were a preparation for the kingdom to come.

Through his words, Peter emphasized the importance of faithfulness and anticipation. The Millennium was not merely a future event but a present call to align one's life with the values of the Messiah's kingdom.

And as Peter continued to proclaim the vision, he prayed that all who heard would set their hearts on the coming reign of the Lamb, living in faith and hope until the day when the earth would be filled with His glory, and His peace would reign forever.

Chapter 28
The Final Judgment

The vision opened with an overwhelming silence, the kind that comes before the breaking of a storm. Peter stood on the edge of eternity, his spirit trembling as he beheld the great and glorious throne of the Creator. It was pure and radiant, its light piercing through the heavens and the earth. Before this throne, all creation gathered, their faces turned toward the Judge of all. This was the Final Judgment—the ultimate reckoning, where every soul would stand before the Creator and give an account.

"This is the hour of truth," the voice said, solemn and resolute. "Here, the deeds of every life are revealed, and justice and mercy are brought to completion."

Peter's gaze was drawn to the throne, where the Messiah sat in glory, His presence a blend of majesty and compassion. The heavens and the earth fled from His face, their imperfections unable to endure His holiness. Yet the faithful stood firm, clothed in the righteousness of the Lamb.

Before the throne was the Book of Life, its pages inscribed with the names of those who had trusted in the Lamb. Another set of books lay open, containing the deeds of all humanity. Peter felt the weight of these books, for they held the record of every thought, word, and action—nothing was hidden, and all was brought into the light.

The vision shifted, and Peter saw the gathering of all nations. Kings and commoners, rich and poor, the mighty and the lowly—all stood as equals before the throne. Their faces reflected a mixture of awe and dread, for none could escape the gaze of the Judge.

The Messiah began to separate them, as a shepherd divides the sheep from the goats. To those on His right, He spoke words of welcome and joy:

"Come, you who are blessed by my Father; inherit the kingdom prepared for you from the foundation of the world."

These were the ones who had fed the hungry, clothed the naked, cared for the sick, and visited the imprisoned. Their acts of love, born out of faith, were the evidence of their allegiance to the Lamb.

To those on His left, however, the words were stark:

"Depart from me, you cursed, into the eternal fire prepared for the devil and his angels."

These were the ones who had ignored the needs of others, their lives consumed by self-interest and indifference. Their rejection of the Creator's love was revealed in their treatment of their fellow humans.

Peter saw the fear and regret in the faces of those who were cast out, their rebellion laid bare before the throne. They pleaded, offering excuses and justifications, yet the truth was undeniable. The choices they had made in life had shaped their eternal destiny.

"This is the justice of my kingdom," the voice said. "Mercy was offered, but they chose to reject it. Their separation is not my will, but their own."

The vision grew more intense as Peter was shown the fate of the Adversary and his followers. Satan, the Beast, the False Prophet, and all who had aligned themselves with darkness were cast into the lake of fire. This was the second death, the final defeat of sin, death, and evil.

"Their rebellion is ended," the voice declared. "No longer will they deceive, destroy, or corrupt. My creation is free, and my justice is complete."

Peter was then shown the reward of the faithful. They were welcomed into the New Jerusalem, their names written in the Book of Life, their tears wiped away by the hand of the

Creator. They walked in the light of the Lamb, their joy eternal and unbroken.

The faithful were not judged by their deeds alone but by their faith in the Messiah. His sacrifice had covered their sins, and His righteousness had become their own.

"This is my mercy," the voice said, filled with love. "To all who believe in my Son, there is no condemnation. They are mine, and I am theirs, forever."

As the vision came to its conclusion, Peter saw the new heaven and the new earth. The old order had passed away, and creation itself was renewed. The throne of the Creator was established at the center, and the faithful dwelled in perfect communion with Him.

"There is no more death, no more mourning, no more pain," the voice declared. "Behold, I make all things new."

When Peter returned from the vision, his heart was overwhelmed by both the gravity and the hope of what he had seen. The Final Judgment was a moment of profound justice and mercy, the ultimate fulfillment of the Creator's plan.

He gathered the faithful and spoke of the vision, his voice steady yet filled with urgency.

"The day of judgment is coming," Peter proclaimed. "Every deed will be revealed, every heart laid bare. Yet for those who trust in the Lamb, there is no fear, only joy. Let us live as those who are ready, loving one another and walking in His light."

Peter's testimony stirred his listeners deeply. Some resolved to live with greater faith and compassion, knowing that their lives would bear eternal significance. Others found comfort in the assurance of the Messiah's mercy, their hope renewed by the promise of eternal life.

Through his words, Peter emphasized the importance of readiness and faithfulness. The Final Judgment was not a moment to dread but a call to live in the light of the Lamb, embracing His love and sharing it with the world.

And as Peter continued to proclaim the vision, he prayed that all who heard would prepare their hearts for the day when they would stand before the throne, ready to hear the words, **"Well done, good and faithful servant. Enter into the joy of your Lord."**

Chapter 29
The Date of the Apocalypse

The vision opened with an image of the heavens, vast and infinite, where stars moved in patterns known only to their Creator. Peter stood amidst this celestial expanse, sensing a profound order beyond human understanding. He felt the weight of time itself, a force woven into creation yet subject to the One who dwells beyond it.

"The hour of the Apocalypse is known to none but me," the voice declared, resonant with authority and mystery. "It will come like a thief in the night, unanticipated by the proud but awaited by the faithful."

Peter's gaze shifted to the earth, where humanity grappled with the enigma of the Apocalypse. He saw scholars pouring over ancient texts, prophets declaring signs, and skeptics scoffing at the notion of an end. The question of when consumed their thoughts, dividing the faithful and distracting the curious.

The voice spoke again, filled with both patience and admonition. "Why do they seek what is not given to them? The times and seasons are mine to command, not theirs to know."

The vision carried Peter through the ages, showing how the question of the Apocalypse's date had shaped human history. He saw the early church, their hearts filled with urgency as they awaited the return of the Messiah. Their lives were marked by faithfulness, their hope resting not in the timing but in the certainty of His coming.

But Peter also saw the dangers of obsession. In every era, some claimed secret knowledge of the date, their predictions sowing fear and confusion. He saw movements rise and fall, their followers left disillusioned when the appointed day passed without event.

"These are the false prophets," the voice said, sorrowful yet resolute. "They claim to speak for me, yet their words lead my people astray. Beware of them, for they are wolves in sheep's clothing."

The vision turned to the signs that would precede the end. Peter saw wars and rumors of wars, famines and earthquakes, the rise of false messiahs and the persecution of the faithful. These signs were not to pinpoint the date but to remind humanity of the need for vigilance.

Peter understood that the signs were both a warning and a comfort—a reminder of the brokenness of the world and the promise of its restoration.

"The signs are the birth pains," the voice explained. "They point to what is to come but do not reveal the hour. My people are called to watch and pray, not to speculate."

Peter was then shown the importance of living in readiness. He saw the faithful going about their daily lives, their hearts attuned to the Creator's will. They worked, loved, and served with the knowledge that the Apocalypse could come at any moment. Their lives were a testimony to the wisdom of preparation over prediction.

"The wise servant does not wait idly," the voice said. "He tends to his household, ensuring that when the master returns, he is found faithful. Blessed are those who live in readiness, for they shall inherit my kingdom."

The vision shifted once more, showing the futility of humanity's attempts to calculate the date. Peter saw astronomers charting the heavens, mathematicians devising complex formulas, and mystics interpreting dreams—all seeking to uncover what the Creator had kept hidden.

Yet even as they labored, the Apocalypse drew closer, unnoticed by those who had placed their faith in their own understanding rather than in the promises of the Lamb.

"The date is not for them to know," the voice declared. "I come at the appointed time, known only to me. Trust in my timing, for it is perfect."

As the vision concluded, Peter was reminded of the simplicity of the call to faith. The Creator did not require His people to know the date but to live in constant readiness, their hearts anchored in trust and hope.

When Peter returned from the vision, his heart was filled with clarity and purpose. He gathered the faithful and shared what he had seen, his voice steady yet urgent.

"The day and the hour are known to none but the Father," Peter proclaimed. "Do not waste your lives in speculation but live in readiness. Be faithful in your work, steadfast in your hope, and unwavering in your love, for He is coming at an hour you do not expect."

Peter's testimony stirred his listeners deeply. Some wept as they realized their preoccupation with signs and dates had distracted them from living faithfully. Others resolved to focus on their walk with the Creator, preparing their hearts for His return.

Through his words, Peter emphasized the importance of trust and vigilance. The date of the Apocalypse was not for humanity to know but to await with faith and hope.

And as Peter continued to proclaim the vision, he prayed that all who heard would live as though the Apocalypse were at hand, their lives marked by the readiness and joy of those who eagerly awaited the return of the Lamb.

Chapter 30
Humanity's Destiny

The vision began with a sweeping panorama of the earth, its beauty mingled with scars of humanity's dominion. Peter saw the great cities, fields of industry, and sprawling wilderness that bore witness to humanity's creativity and destruction alike. The voice spoke, filled with both sorrow and hope:

"This is the destiny of humanity—a path shaped by their choices, yet guided by my eternal plan. I call them to life, but many choose death. I offer them peace, but many sow strife."

Peter's gaze was drawn to a timeline of human history, flowing like a mighty river. He saw its beginnings in the garden, where humanity walked with the Creator in unbroken fellowship. The river then darkened as sin entered the world, its waters tainted by rebellion and disobedience. Wars, empires, and revolutions churned its flow, reflecting the struggle of humanity to find purpose apart from the Creator.

Yet even in the darkest moments, Peter saw glimmers of hope—figures who stood as beacons of light, prophets and martyrs who called their generation back to the Creator's will. The river, though troubled, moved inevitably toward a glorious horizon.

"The destiny of humanity is not destruction," the voice said, "but redemption. Though many stray, my plan will not be thwarted. I am the Alpha and the Omega, and my purposes shall prevail."

Peter was shown two distinct paths that humanity could follow. One path was broad and well-trodden, its travelers consumed by self-interest and worldly pursuits. This road led to destruction, its end marked by separation from the Creator and the loss of eternal life.

The other path was narrow, winding upward through trials and tribulations. Its travelers bore the marks of faith, their eyes fixed on the light ahead. This road led to the eternal kingdom, where the faithful would dwell with the Creator forever.

"Behold," the voice said, "I set before them life and death, blessings and curses. I call them to choose life, that they may live."

The vision shifted to humanity's achievements—monuments of art, science, and philosophy that reflected the Creator's image in their creativity. Peter saw cathedrals built to glorify God, works of literature that inspired the soul, and discoveries that unlocked the mysteries of creation.

Yet alongside these achievements, he saw the misuse of knowledge and power. Weapons of war, systems of oppression, and ideologies that denied the Creator's existence stood as monuments to humanity's pride.

"The gifts I give are meant to build, not destroy," the voice said. "When humanity walks in my ways, they reflect my glory. When they turn from me, their gifts become tools of their own ruin."

Peter was then shown the culmination of humanity's destiny. He saw the New Jerusalem, its gates open to all who had walked the narrow path. The faithful entered with joy, their lives a testament to the Creator's grace and mercy.

But Peter also saw those who stood outside, their faces marked by regret. They had chosen the broad path, rejecting the light in favor of darkness. Though the gates remained open, their hearts would not turn, and their separation was complete.

"Their destiny is their choice," the voice said, filled with sorrow. "I call to them even now, but they refuse to listen. My mercy endures, yet justice must prevail."

The vision turned to the role of the Messiah in shaping humanity's destiny. Peter saw the cross and the empty tomb, the pivotal moments where death was defeated and hope restored.

The Messiah's sacrifice was the bridge that spanned the chasm between humanity and the Creator, offering a way for all to walk the path of life.

"All who come to my Son shall live," the voice declared. "Through Him, the destiny of humanity is secured, and the promise of eternal life is fulfilled."

As the vision concluded, Peter was shown the final destiny of creation. The earth was renewed, its scars healed, and its beauty restored. Humanity, redeemed and united, walked with the Creator as they had in the beginning.

"This is my plan," the voice said. "Not destruction, but restoration. Not despair, but hope. My purposes are good, and my love endures forever."

When Peter returned from the vision, his heart was heavy with the weight of humanity's choices yet lifted by the promise of the Creator's plan. He gathered the faithful and spoke of the vision, his voice steady yet filled with passion.

"Humanity's destiny is in the hands of the Creator," Peter proclaimed. "He calls us to life, offering hope through His Son. Choose the narrow path, for it leads to joy eternal. Reject the broad way, for its end is destruction. Live as those who bear the image of God, reflecting His love and truth in all you do."

Peter's words stirred his listeners deeply. Some reflected on the path they were walking, resolving to align their lives with the Creator's will. Others rejoiced in the assurance of the Messiah's victory, their hope renewed by the vision of restoration.

Through his testimony, Peter emphasized the importance of choice and responsibility. Humanity's destiny was not a matter of chance but of deliberate action, shaped by the decisions of each individual.

And as Peter continued to proclaim the vision, he prayed that all who heard would choose the path of life, walking in faith, hope, and love until the day when humanity's destiny would be fully realized in the eternal kingdom of the Creator.

Chapter 31
Salvation

The vision unfolded with a brilliance that seemed to encompass both the vastness of the heavens and the intimacy of a single human soul. Peter stood at the crossroads of humanity's greatest longing: salvation—the promise of deliverance from sin and restoration to communion with the Creator.

"This is my gift," the voice said, resonant with both tenderness and authority. "Salvation is not earned but given, not achieved but received. It is my love poured out for the world."

Peter was drawn to the image of a shepherd tenderly carrying a lost lamb. The lamb, weary and frightened, bore the marks of its wandering, yet the shepherd's grip was firm, his gaze filled with joy.

"This is the heart of salvation," the voice explained. "I seek the lost, and I rejoice when they are found. It is not my will that any should perish, but that all should come to repentance."

The vision expanded to reveal the history of salvation, beginning in the garden where humanity's fall had introduced sin and death. Peter saw the Creator's unbroken pursuit of His creation, even as they turned away.

He witnessed the call of Abraham, the covenant with Israel, the law given to Moses, and the voices of the prophets—all threads in the tapestry of salvation. Each moment pointed toward the coming of the Messiah, the Lamb who would take away the sins of the world.

"The plan of salvation was established before the foundation of the earth," the voice said. "Through my Son, the way is opened for all who believe."

Peter was shown the cross, the pinnacle of salvation's story. He saw the Messiah's suffering, His body broken and His blood poured out. Yet he also saw the triumph of the empty tomb, where death was defeated, and life eternal was secured.

"The cross is the bridge," the voice said, filled with both sorrow and joy. "Through it, my justice and mercy meet. My Son bore the weight of sin so that humanity might be free."

The vision turned to the present, where Peter saw the call of salvation being proclaimed across the earth. He witnessed preachers and missionaries sharing the message of the Gospel, their words reaching hearts in every nation, tribe, and tongue.

Peter also saw the struggles of those who resisted the call, their hearts burdened by doubt, pride, or fear. Yet the Spirit continued to work, softening hearts and drawing them toward the Creator's love.

"My salvation is for all," the voice declared. "To the weary and burdened, I give rest. To the broken and contrite, I give healing. Let all who thirst come and drink freely."

The vision shifted to the varied beliefs about salvation that existed among humanity. Peter saw those who sought salvation through their own efforts, striving to earn favor through good works or religious rituals. Others placed their hope in philosophies or ideologies, seeking meaning apart from the Creator.

Yet amid these attempts, Peter saw the simplicity and power of the Gospel. Salvation was not the result of human effort but the gift of grace, received through faith in the Messiah.

"It is by grace you are saved," the voice said, firm yet gentle. "Not of works, lest anyone should boast. My salvation is a gift, offered freely to all who believe."

Peter's heart swelled as he was shown the fruits of salvation in the lives of the faithful. He saw lives transformed, relationships restored, and communities healed. The power of sin was broken, and the light of the Creator shone through those who had been redeemed.

Yet Peter also saw the cost of rejecting salvation. Those who turned away from the Creator's gift remained bound by sin, their separation from Him a source of eternal sorrow.

"I do not force my gift upon anyone," the voice said, sorrowful yet resolute. "The choice is theirs. Yet even to the last moment, my mercy endures, and my call remains."

As the vision concluded, Peter saw the culmination of salvation in the New Jerusalem. The faithful, redeemed by the blood of the Lamb, walked in perfect communion with the Creator. Their tears were wiped away, their sorrows turned to joy, and their lives a testimony to the greatness of His love.

"This is the end of salvation's story," the voice declared. "My people with me, and I with them, forever."

When Peter returned from the vision, his heart burned with both urgency and hope. Salvation was not merely a theological concept but the Creator's greatest gift—a bridge from death to life, from despair to hope.

He gathered the faithful and spoke of the vision, his voice steady yet filled with passion.

"Salvation is offered to all," Peter proclaimed. "It is the gift of the Creator's grace, received through faith in the Lamb. Do not delay, for today is the day of salvation. Open your hearts to His love and walk in the light of His redemption."

Peter's testimony stirred his listeners deeply. Some wept with gratitude, their hearts overwhelmed by the assurance of the Messiah's sacrifice. Others resolved to share the message of salvation with those who had not yet heard, their spirits ignited by the vision's urgency.

Through his words, Peter emphasized the simplicity and power of salvation. It was not a reward for the righteous but a gift for the repentant, a call to trust in the One who had given His life for the world.

And as Peter continued to proclaim the vision, he prayed that all who heard would embrace the gift of salvation, walking in faith, hope, and love until the day they stood before the Creator, redeemed and restored for eternity.

Chapter 32
Free Will

The vision began with a scene of humanity at a crossroads, where paths stretched infinitely in all directions. Each path represented a choice, and every choice carried consequences. Peter stood among the multitudes, watching as individuals paused to consider their options, some choosing wisely, others veering toward paths of destruction.

"This is the gift of free will," the voice declared, resonant with both gravity and love. "It is the power to choose, a reflection of my image within humanity. Yet with this gift comes great responsibility."

Peter's gaze was drawn to the garden of Eden, where the first choice was made. He saw Adam and Eve standing before the Tree of the Knowledge of Good and Evil, their hearts filled with innocence yet swayed by the serpent's lies.

"The choice was theirs," the voice explained. "I did not compel their obedience, for love cannot exist without freedom. Yet their choice brought sin and death into the world."

Peter saw how this first act of rebellion had set the stage for humanity's ongoing struggle. The gift of free will, meant for good, became a double-edged sword—offering the potential for both righteousness and ruin.

The vision shifted to reveal the vast array of choices faced by humanity. Peter saw moments of self-sacrifice, acts of kindness, and decisions that brought healing and hope. He also saw greed, cruelty, and betrayal, choices that tore at the fabric of relationships and communities.

"The power to choose is sacred," the voice said. "Through it, humanity shapes its destiny. I offer guidance, but I do not coerce. My Spirit whispers, but the heart must respond."

Peter was shown how free will played a role in salvation. He saw the Creator's hand extended to humanity, offering the gift of grace through the Messiah. Yet this gift required a response—a choice to accept or reject the love that was freely given.

"The door is open," the voice declared. "But each must decide to enter. I will not force my love upon anyone, for love that is compelled is no love at all."

Peter watched as some embraced the gift of salvation, their hearts transformed by faith. Others turned away, their pride or fear preventing them from accepting what was offered.

The vision turned to the consequences of humanity's choices. Peter saw the ripple effects of decisions, how one act of kindness could inspire a chain of good, while one act of cruelty could unleash waves of suffering. He understood that free will was not isolated but interconnected, each choice impacting others in ways seen and unseen.

"Every choice matters," the voice said. "No act of love is too small, no sin too hidden to escape its consequences. Yet my grace is sufficient to redeem even the darkest path."

Peter was then shown the Creator's role in guiding free will. He saw how the Spirit worked within the hearts of humanity, offering wisdom and conviction. He witnessed moments where the Spirit's prompting turned individuals away from destruction, leading them toward life.

Yet Peter also saw the pain of rejection—the Creator's sorrow as humanity chose paths that led away from Him.

"I do not abandon those who stray," the voice said, filled with both sadness and hope. "I pursue them, calling them back to me. Yet the choice remains theirs."

The vision revealed how free will shaped the relationship between humanity and the Creator. Peter saw how trust and love flourished in the absence of compulsion, how the Creator's desire was not for servitude but for communion.

"The greatest commandment is to love me with all your heart, soul, and mind," the voice said. "Yet love must be given freely, not taken by force. This is the beauty and the burden of free will."

As the vision concluded, Peter was shown the eternal implications of free will. Those who chose the path of the Lamb entered into eternal life, their decisions reflecting their faith and love. Those who rejected the Creator faced separation, their choices leading them away from the light.

"Free will is my gift and my test," the voice said. "Through it, the heart is revealed, and eternity is shaped. Choose wisely, for the stakes are eternal."

When Peter returned from the vision, his heart was filled with both awe and urgency. Free will was not merely a philosophical concept but a divine gift, a reflection of the Creator's image and a means of shaping one's destiny.

He gathered the faithful and spoke of the vision, his voice steady yet filled with passion.

"Free will is the gift of the Creator," Peter proclaimed. "Through it, we choose whom we will serve. Let us choose the path of life, walking in obedience and love, for our choices echo into eternity. Seek His guidance, trust in His Spirit, and let your decisions reflect His glory."

Peter's testimony stirred his listeners deeply. Some reflected on the weight of their choices, resolving to align their lives with the Creator's will. Others found hope in the assurance that even their past mistakes could be redeemed through grace.

Through his words, Peter emphasized the sacredness of free will and the responsibility it carried. It was not a burden but an opportunity—a chance to reflect the Creator's love through every decision.

And as Peter continued to proclaim the vision, he prayed that all who heard would choose wisely, embracing the gift of free will as a means to draw closer to the Creator and walk the path of eternal life.

Chapter 33
Original Sin

The vision opened with a vivid return to the garden of Eden, where the perfection of creation surrounded Peter. The trees were lush, the rivers pure, and the air carried the unmistakable presence of the Creator. At the center of this paradise stood the Tree of the Knowledge of Good and Evil, its fruit radiant and inviting, yet marked by an invisible warning.

"This is where it began," the voice said, resonant with sorrow and truth. "The choice made here rippled through all creation, introducing sin and death into what I had declared very good."

Peter saw Adam and Eve, clothed in innocence, their faces alight with the wonder of the world entrusted to them. Yet their gaze was drawn to the forbidden tree, where the serpent spoke words laced with cunning and deceit.

"Did God really say...?" the serpent whispered, its voice a seed of doubt. It painted disobedience as wisdom, rebellion as freedom, and sin as a path to divinity.

Peter's heart ached as he witnessed their choice. They reached for the fruit, their hands trembling, their decision a tragic turning point for all humanity. The moment they ate, a shadow fell over the garden, and Peter felt the weight of their disobedience.

"This is original sin," the voice declared. "It is the first fracture, the breaking of trust between Creator and creation. Through this, sin entered the world, and with it, death."

The vision expanded, showing Peter the consequences of that single act. He saw Cain raising his hand against Abel, the first murder staining the earth with innocent blood. He witnessed the spread of corruption, humanity's thoughts and actions turning continually toward evil.

Peter saw the tower of Babel rise as a monument to pride, the floodwaters consuming a world consumed by wickedness, and Sodom and Gomorrah reduced to ashes by their rebellion. Each event was a manifestation of original sin, its corruption passed down through generations.

"Through one man, sin entered the world," the voice said, heavy with sorrow. "And death through sin. Thus, death spread to all men, for all have sinned."

Peter's spirit was drawn deeper into the nature of original sin. He saw how it was not merely an act but a condition—a distortion of the soul that separated humanity from the Creator. The hearts of men and women were inclined toward selfishness and rebellion, their desires often at odds with the Creator's will.

"The image of God remains," the voice explained, "but it is marred, like a mirror cracked and dimmed. Humanity was created for communion with me, but sin has severed that bond."

The vision turned to the law given to Moses, where the Creator sought to guide humanity back to righteousness. Peter saw the commandments etched in stone, a reflection of the Creator's holiness and justice.

Yet even as the law was given, Peter saw its limitations. It revealed sin but could not remove it. The sacrifices of bulls and goats were insufficient to cleanse the stain of original sin.

"The law is a tutor," the voice said, "pointing to the need for a Savior. It shows the depth of humanity's need and the height of my mercy."

Peter's gaze shifted to the cross, where the weight of original sin was borne by the Messiah. He saw the Lamb of God, bruised and broken, yet triumphant in His sacrifice. Through His death and resurrection, the power of sin was broken, and the way to reconciliation was opened.

"Through one man, sin entered," the voice declared, "but through one man, righteousness abounds. My Son has undone what was broken in the garden, offering life to all who believe."

The vision revealed the ongoing struggle with sin, even for the redeemed. Peter saw how the remnants of original sin lingered, tempting the faithful and waging war against their spirits. Yet he also saw the power of grace, the Spirit working within to transform hearts and restore the image of the Creator.

"This is sanctification," the voice explained. "Though sin's power is broken, its presence remains. My Spirit is the fire that refines, purifying my people until they are made whole."

As the vision concluded, Peter was shown the final defeat of sin. He saw the New Jerusalem, where the curse was no more and the faithful walked in perfect communion with the Creator. The mirror, once cracked, was restored, reflecting His glory in full.

"This is my promise," the voice said. "Sin shall not have the final word. My grace is sufficient, and my love endures forever."

When Peter returned from the vision, his heart was heavy with the weight of humanity's fall yet filled with hope in the Messiah's redemption. He gathered the faithful and spoke of what he had seen, his voice steady yet urgent.

"Original sin is the root of all brokenness," Peter proclaimed. "It is the inheritance of our first parents, a stain we cannot remove on our own. Yet the Lamb has borne its weight, offering grace to all who repent. Let us turn to Him, trusting in His sacrifice and walking in the light of His Spirit."

Peter's testimony stirred his listeners deeply. Some wept with gratitude for the forgiveness offered through the Messiah, while others resolved to walk more faithfully, knowing the ongoing struggle against sin.

Through his words, Peter emphasized the reality of original sin and the hope found in the Creator's redemptive plan. Sin was not the end of humanity's story but the beginning of grace's triumph.

And as Peter continued to proclaim the vision, he prayed that all who heard would embrace the gift of grace, allowing the

Spirit to transform their hearts and restore them to the fullness of the Creator's image.

Chapter 34
Divine Grace

The vision opened with a radiant light that enveloped Peter, brighter than the sun yet gentle as a loving embrace. He stood in awe as the light revealed a stream of pure water flowing from the throne of the Creator, its currents shimmering with life and mercy. This was Divine Grace—unearned, inexhaustible, and freely given to humanity.

"This is my grace," the voice declared, filled with tenderness and authority. "It is my love poured out for the undeserving, my strength made perfect in weakness, and the bridge that restores my children to me."

Peter was drawn to the stream, his spirit overwhelmed by its purity. The water seemed alive, carrying the essence of the Creator's love. He saw how it flowed to the ends of the earth, reaching even the most desolate and broken places.

"No heart is too hardened, no soul too lost," the voice said. "My grace is sufficient for all. It seeks, it saves, and it restores."

The vision shifted, and Peter was shown humanity's need for grace. He saw individuals weighed down by guilt and shame, their lives fractured by sin. Some labored tirelessly, attempting to earn favor through good deeds, while others despaired, believing themselves beyond redemption.

"My grace is not earned," the voice explained. "It is a gift, given freely to those who receive it. It is not by works but by faith that my children are made whole."

Peter's gaze turned to the cross, where the fullness of grace was revealed. He saw the Messiah, His arms stretched wide, bearing the weight of humanity's sin. Through His sacrifice, the chasm between Creator and creation was bridged, and the gift of grace was extended to all.

"This is the fountain of grace," the voice said, filled with both sorrow and triumph. "My Son gave His life so that you might live. Through His blood, my grace flows without end."

Peter was then shown the transformative power of grace in the lives of the faithful. He saw broken relationships restored, chains of addiction shattered, and hearts of stone replaced with hearts of flesh. Grace was not a passive gift but an active force, renewing and empowering those who embraced it.

"My grace does not leave you as you are," the voice declared. "It calls you to grow, to become more like my Son. It is the fire that refines and the balm that heals."

The vision expanded to include the community of believers, bound together by the grace they had received. Peter saw them extending grace to one another, forgiving offenses, and bearing each other's burdens. Through their love and unity, the light of the Creator shone brightly, drawing others into the fold.

"As I have forgiven you, so you must forgive one another," the voice said. "My grace is not yours to hoard but to share. Through it, the world will know that you are mine."

Peter was shown how grace sustained the faithful through trials and hardships. He saw individuals enduring persecution, their strength renewed by the Spirit. He witnessed moments of weakness transformed into testimonies of divine power.

"My grace is sufficient," the voice said, firm yet comforting. "In your weakness, my strength is made perfect. Trust in me, and you will find all you need."

As the vision concluded, Peter saw the ultimate fulfillment of grace in the New Jerusalem. The faithful stood before the throne, their robes washed white in the blood of the Lamb. There was no more guilt, no more shame, only joy and peace in the presence of the Creator.

"This is the end of grace's work," the voice declared. "My children restored, my creation renewed, and my love made complete."

When Peter returned from the vision, his heart overflowed with gratitude and awe. Divine Grace was not only the foundation of salvation but the ongoing power that sustained and transformed the faithful.

He gathered the believers and spoke of the vision, his voice steady yet filled with wonder.

"Grace is the gift of the Creator," Peter proclaimed. "It is unearned, unstoppable, and unfailing. Let us receive it with humble hearts and live as those transformed by His love. Extend grace to one another, for in doing so, you reflect the heart of the Creator."

Peter's testimony stirred his listeners deeply. Some wept with gratitude for the grace that had lifted them from the depths of despair. Others resolved to extend grace to those who had wronged them, committing to live as vessels of the Creator's love.

Through his words, Peter emphasized the transformative and boundless nature of Divine Grace. It was not a mere concept but a living reality, a force that reached into the darkest places and brought light.

And as Peter continued to proclaim the vision, he prayed that all who heard would embrace the gift of grace, allowing it to renew their hearts, restore their relationships, and draw them ever closer to the Creator, whose love knows no bounds.

Chapter 35
The Resurrection of the Dead

The vision unfolded with a stirring stillness, as though the very fabric of creation awaited a monumental event. Peter stood on a vast plain where the earth seemed to shimmer with expectation. Suddenly, a sound like a trumpet echoed across the heavens, and the ground trembled beneath him. This was the resurrection of the dead—the moment when the graves would open, and life would conquer death.

"This is my promise," the voice declared, filled with majesty and assurance. "As my Son rose, so shall all who are in Him. Death is not the end but the threshold of eternity."

Peter's gaze turned to the horizon, where he saw graves bursting open. From the dust emerged men and women, their forms transformed, their bodies radiant with new life. These were the righteous, those whose faith had been in the Creator. Their faces shone with joy as they were reunited with loved ones and drawn into the light of the Lamb.

"The perishable is clothed with the imperishable," the voice said. "The mortal is swallowed up by life. This is the victory of my Son, the defeat of the last enemy—death itself."

Peter was shown the resurrection of the righteous in its fullness. Their bodies, once frail and broken, were now incorruptible, reflecting the glory of the Creator. There was no sickness, no pain, no scars—only perfection, as they were made new in His image.

"They are my children," the voice continued. "Through their faith, they have been justified, and now they share in the resurrection of my Son. This is the fulfillment of the hope they carried in their hearts."

The vision shifted, revealing the resurrection of the unrighteous. Peter saw those who had rejected the Creator's call rising to face judgment. Their bodies, too, were restored, but their faces bore the weight of regret and fear. They stood before the throne, their deeds revealed, their hearts laid bare.

"This is the resurrection of judgment," the voice said, heavy with sorrow. "I gave them life, I offered them mercy, yet they chose the path of rebellion. My justice is perfect, and their separation is their choice."

Peter was shown how the resurrection connected to the Messiah's triumph over death. He saw the empty tomb, the stone rolled away, and the risen Christ appearing to His followers. The power that raised the Messiah from the dead was the same power now bringing life to all who believed.

"My Son is the firstfruits of the resurrection," the voice declared. "Through Him, the gates of death are broken, and the promise of eternal life is made sure."

Peter's spirit was drawn to the faithful who had lived in anticipation of this moment. He saw martyrs who had laid down their lives for their faith, their sacrifices now crowned with glory. He saw saints who had endured trials and temptations, their perseverance rewarded with eternal joy.

"They overcame by the blood of the Lamb and the word of their testimony," the voice said. "Their tears are wiped away, their sorrows turned to joy, for they now dwell with me forever."

The vision revealed the culmination of the resurrection in the New Jerusalem. Peter saw the faithful gathered before the throne, their voices lifting in songs of praise. They walked in perfect communion with the Creator, their lives a reflection of His love and glory.

"This is the inheritance of my people," the voice said. "Eternal life in my presence, where death and sorrow are no more."

As the vision concluded, Peter was shown the significance of the resurrection for the present. It was not merely a future hope but a transformative truth that shaped how the faithful lived. He saw individuals facing trials with courage, their faith anchored in the certainty of the resurrection.

"The resurrection is the foundation of your hope," the voice said. "Live as those who will rise, for your life is hidden with Christ in me."

When Peter returned from the vision, his heart was filled with both awe and joy. The resurrection of the dead was not only a promise but a reality secured by the victory of the Messiah.

He gathered the faithful and spoke of the vision, his voice steady yet filled with passion.

"The resurrection is our hope," Peter proclaimed. "Through the Messiah, death has lost its sting, and the grave its victory. Live in this truth, for you are destined for eternal life. Let this hope shape your days, strengthen your hearts, and guide your steps."

Peter's testimony stirred his listeners deeply. Some wept with joy, their grief for lost loved ones transformed by the promise of reunion. Others resolved to live with greater purpose, knowing that their lives carried eternal significance.

Through his words, Peter emphasized the power and promise of the resurrection. It was not merely an event to anticipate but a truth that gave meaning and strength to every moment of life.

And as Peter continued to proclaim the vision, he prayed that all who heard would embrace the hope of the resurrection, living in the light of eternity and the assurance of life in the presence of the Creator forever.

Chapter 36
Heaven and Hell

The vision opened with a stark contrast, as Peter stood at the crossroads of eternity. On one side lay Heaven, radiant with the glory of the Creator, a place of joy and peace beyond human comprehension. On the other side loomed Hell, a realm of despair and separation, its darkness a chilling reflection of rebellion's consequence.

"This is the destiny of all souls," the voice declared, resonant with both love and justice. "Heaven is the reward of the faithful, and Hell the consequence of rejection. My mercy calls to all, but the choice is theirs."

Peter's gaze was drawn first to Heaven, where the gates of the New Jerusalem stood open. Beyond them, he saw a city of incomparable beauty, its streets paved with gold like transparent glass, its walls adorned with every precious stone. The River of Life flowed from the throne of the Creator, and the Tree of Life stood on its banks, bearing fruit in every season.

The faithful moved freely within this paradise, their faces radiant with joy. Their songs of praise filled the air, a harmony that resonated with the Creator's glory.

"This is the dwelling place of my people," the voice said, tender and joyful. "Here, they will see my face and know me as I know them. There is no more pain, no more death, for the former things have passed away."

The vision shifted to reveal the purpose of Heaven beyond its beauty. Peter saw the faithful engaged in worship, not as a passive act but as a dynamic expression of their love and gratitude. Some sang, others danced, and still others worked joyfully, their labors an act of devotion.

"Heaven is not idleness," the voice explained. "It is the fulfillment of purpose, the restoration of communion, and the celebration of my eternal love."

Peter saw how Heaven was not merely a reward but a relationship—a place where the Creator's presence was the source of every joy, every desire fulfilled in Him alone.

Peter's attention turned to Hell, and his heart grew heavy with the sorrow of what he saw. The realm was dark and desolate, its landscape barren and lifeless. Souls wandered, burdened by the weight of their choices, their separation from the Creator a torment greater than any physical pain.

"This is Hell," the voice said, solemn and unyielding. "It is the absence of my presence, the consequence of a life lived in rebellion. I take no pleasure in this, yet my justice cannot be denied."

Peter was shown the nature of Hell's suffering. It was not imposed but self-inflicted, a reflection of each soul's rejection of the Creator's love. He saw individuals consumed by regret, their hearts burdened by the realization of what they had lost.

"They chose darkness over light," the voice said. "Their separation is not my will but their own. Even now, my mercy calls to the living, that they might turn and be saved."

The vision revealed the connection between Heaven and Hell and the choices made in life. Peter saw how small decisions—acts of kindness or cruelty, moments of faith or defiance—shaped the trajectory of each soul. He understood that Heaven and Hell were not arbitrary destinations but the culmination of a life's direction.

"The path is narrow that leads to life," the voice said, "and few find it. Yet my call is unceasing, and my grace sufficient for all who turn to me."

Peter was then shown the Creator's heart for humanity. He saw how the gates of Heaven remained open, a testament to the Creator's longing for all to enter. He also saw the sorrow in the Creator's face as souls chose to walk away, their rejection a wound borne in divine love.

"I desire that none should perish," the voice declared. "But love must be chosen, and I will not compel it. To those who seek me, I give eternal life. To those who reject me, I honor their choice."

As the vision concluded, Peter was shown the eternal joy of Heaven and the eternal sorrow of Hell. The faithful walked in the light of the Lamb, their lives a celebration of the Creator's love. The lost remained in darkness, their separation a reminder of the cost of rebellion.

"This is the truth of eternity," the voice said. "Heaven for those who are mine, Hell for those who reject me. Choose life, that you may live."

When Peter returned from the vision, his heart was filled with both urgency and hope. Heaven and Hell were not mere concepts but realities that demanded a response.

He gathered the faithful and spoke of what he had seen, his voice steady yet filled with passion.

"Heaven is the dwelling place of the faithful," Peter proclaimed. "It is the joy of eternal communion with the Creator. Hell is the separation of the soul from its source of life. Let us choose the path that leads to life, walking in faith and obedience to the Lamb. His mercy is extended to all—embrace it and live."

Peter's testimony stirred his listeners deeply. Some reflected on their lives, resolving to align their hearts with the Creator's will. Others wept with gratitude for the assurance of Heaven and the invitation to share its joy.

Through his words, Peter emphasized the reality and significance of Heaven and Hell. These were not abstract ideas but the ultimate destinations of every soul, shaped by the choices made in life.

And as Peter continued to proclaim the vision, he prayed that all who heard would choose the light of Heaven, walking the narrow path that led to eternal joy and rejecting the darkness of Hell, where separation from the Creator was the greatest sorrow of all.

Chapter 37
Life After Death

The vision began in a realm of transition, where the boundaries between the physical and spiritual blurred into a luminous veil. Peter stood amidst an ethereal expanse, where souls passed from the temporal to the eternal. The questions of life after death weighed heavily, as he observed the fate of humanity beyond the final breath.

"This is the mystery revealed," the voice declared, both tender and authoritative. "Death is not the end but a doorway. Through it, every soul enters eternity, where their choices and faith are brought to fruition."

Peter's gaze turned to those who had departed this life. He saw the righteous carried by angels into the presence of the Creator, their faces radiant with joy. These were the faithful who had walked with the Lamb, their lives reflecting His light. They entered a realm of peace and rest, their burdens left behind, their hearts filled with eternal hope.

"To those who die in me," the voice said, "there is no death, only life everlasting. They are with me where I am, and nothing shall separate them from my love."

The vision shifted to reveal the state of those who had rejected the Creator's call. Peter saw them entering a shadowed realm, their faces marked by regret and fear. They wandered in the absence of light, burdened by the weight of their choices, yet still within reach of the Creator's mercy.

"Even here, my call endures," the voice said, sorrowful yet resolute. "For those who turn to me, my grace is sufficient. Yet many cling to their pride, refusing the life I offer."

Peter was then shown the connection between life on earth and the eternal state of the soul. He saw how the choices made in the temporal shaped the destiny of the eternal. Acts of love, faith, and obedience created a foundation for everlasting joy, while rebellion, apathy, and selfishness led to separation and sorrow.

"Life is a preparation for eternity," the voice explained. "Every moment is a gift, every choice an echo in eternity. I call humanity to live with this in their hearts, to walk the path of life that leads to me."

The vision deepened as Peter was shown the role of the Messiah in life after death. He saw the Lamb standing at the threshold of eternity, His arms open to receive all who came to Him. Through His death and resurrection, He had removed the sting of death, transforming it into a passageway to life.

"My Son has triumphed over death," the voice declared. "Through Him, the gates of eternity are open to all who believe. In Him is the promise of resurrection and the assurance of eternal life."

Peter witnessed the reality of life after death for the faithful. He saw them dwelling in the presence of the Creator, their lives filled with purpose and joy. They worshiped with abandon, explored the wonders of the new creation, and experienced the fullness of communion with the Almighty.

"This is the promise fulfilled," the voice said. "No eye has seen, no ear has heard, no heart has imagined the things I have prepared for those who love me. This is the joy of eternal life."

The vision turned to the final separation of the righteous and the wicked. Peter saw the Great White Throne, where every soul stood before the Creator. The righteous entered into eternal joy, while the wicked, having chosen separation, faced the consequences of their rebellion.

"Life after death is a reality for all," the voice said. "To the faithful, it is life eternal in my presence. To the unrepentant, it is existence apart from me, a consequence of their choice. My justice is perfect, and my mercy endures, but the choice must be made in life."

As the vision concluded, Peter was shown the hope of the resurrection. He saw graves opening and the faithful rising, their bodies transformed and united with their souls. They entered into the new heaven and new earth, where death and sorrow were no more.

"This is the culmination of my plan," the voice declared. "Life unending, joy unbroken, and communion restored. Death is swallowed up in victory."

When Peter returned from the vision, his heart was filled with both urgency and hope. Life after death was not a mystery to be feared but a promise to be embraced.

He gathered the faithful and spoke of what he had seen, his voice steady yet filled with passion.

"Life after death is the reality of eternity," Peter proclaimed. "Through the Lamb, we have the assurance of life in the presence of the Creator. Let us live with this hope, walking in faith and preparing our hearts for the day we step into His eternal light. Death is not the end—it is the beginning."

Peter's testimony stirred his listeners deeply. Some found comfort in the promise of reunion with loved ones who had gone before them. Others resolved to live more faithfully, knowing that their actions carried eternal significance.

Through his words, Peter emphasized the hope and responsibility of life after death. It was not merely a continuation but a fulfillment—a moment when all that had been promised would be realized.

And as Peter continued to proclaim the vision, he prayed that all who heard would live in the light of eternity, embracing the assurance of life after death and the joy of dwelling forever in the presence of the Creator.

Chapter 38
Reincarnation

The vision unfolded with an air of curiosity and wonder. Peter stood in a space where humanity's deepest questions about existence and eternity converged. Before him, the concept of reincarnation was presented—not as truth, but as a belief held by many seeking to understand the mystery of life, death, and the soul's journey.

"This is the path some believe," the voice said, filled with compassion and clarity. "Yet my truth is not found in cycles but in redemption. I offer not repetition, but renewal and eternal life."

Peter's gaze turned to scenes of humanity's search for meaning. He saw individuals across ages and cultures wrestling with the impermanence of life. Reincarnation appeared as an attempt to reconcile life's brevity with the soul's longing for eternity. It was a belief that promised second chances, where the soul could learn and grow through successive lifetimes.

"The heart seeks understanding," the voice said. "But my ways are higher than their ways, and my truth surpasses their imaginations. Reincarnation is a reflection of their desire for purpose, yet it does not reveal the fullness of my plan."

The vision shifted to the Creator's design for the soul. Peter saw the moment of humanity's creation, where life was breathed into Adam, making him a living being. He witnessed the unique and irreplaceable nature of each soul, crafted in the image of the Creator and imbued with eternal significance.

"Each soul is precious," the voice declared. "I have numbered the hairs on their heads and written their names on the palms of my hands. Their lives are not cycles but stories, each one a part of my eternal tapestry."

Peter was shown the limitations of reincarnation as a belief. He saw individuals burdened by the weight of past lives, striving endlessly for perfection without assurance of redemption. The cycles offered no clear path to reconciliation with the Creator, leaving the soul in a perpetual search for meaning.

"My grace is sufficient," the voice said, firm yet tender. "There is no need for endless cycles. Through my Son, I have made all things new. One life is enough when it is lived in me."

The vision turned to the Gospel's response to reincarnation. Peter saw the Messiah, His arms stretched wide on the cross, bearing the sins of humanity. His sacrifice was final, offering complete redemption and the promise of eternal life to all who believed.

"Reincarnation cannot cleanse sin," the voice declared. "Only the blood of the Lamb can do that. In Him, there is no need for striving, for salvation is a gift freely given to all who receive it."

Peter was shown the promise of resurrection as the Creator's answer to the soul's longing for eternity. He saw the faithful rising at the sound of the trumpet, their bodies transformed and their souls reunited with the Creator. This was not a cycle of returning but a glorious culmination, where the soul entered into its eternal home.

"My plan is not repetition but restoration," the voice said. "Through the resurrection, death is defeated, and life is eternal. This is the destiny I offer to all who come to me."

The vision revealed how the belief in reincarnation could serve as a stepping stone for some to seek deeper truths. Peter saw individuals who, while searching for meaning through reincarnation, eventually encountered the Gospel and embraced the Creator's promise of eternal life.

"I meet them where they are," the voice said, filled with compassion. "Their search for meaning is not ignored, but I call them beyond it. I lead them to the truth, where their questions find their answer in me."

As the vision concluded, Peter was reminded of the Creator's invitation to all humanity. Reincarnation reflected the soul's longing for hope and growth, but it was incomplete without the truth of the Messiah's redemption.

"This is my call," the voice declared. "Come to me, all who labor and are heavy laden, and I will give you rest. In me, the search ends, and life eternal begins."

When Peter returned from the vision, his heart was filled with compassion for those who sought meaning through reincarnation. He gathered the faithful and spoke of what he had seen, his voice steady yet filled with understanding.

"Reincarnation is a reflection of humanity's longing for eternity," Peter proclaimed. "Yet it falls short of the truth revealed in the Messiah. Through Him, we are offered not cycles but a single, eternal destiny with the Creator. Embrace His gift of life, and you will find rest for your soul."

Peter's testimony stirred his listeners deeply. Some reflected on their own searches for meaning, finding assurance in the Gospel's promise of redemption. Others resolved to share the truth with those who held beliefs in reincarnation, offering the hope of eternal life through the Lamb.

Through his words, Peter emphasized the Creator's desire for each soul to find its home in Him. The search for meaning was not to be condemned but fulfilled in the truth of the Gospel.

And as Peter continued to proclaim the vision, he prayed that all who heard would embrace the Creator's promise, stepping away from the cycle of uncertainty and into the certainty of eternal life in His presence.

Chapter 39
Purgatory

The vision unfolded in a realm of paradox, a space where light and shadow intertwined, where souls appeared suspended between the temporal and the eternal. Peter stood amidst this ethereal expanse, his spirit heavy with the weight of what lay before him. This was the concept of Purgatory, a belief held by many as an intermediate state where souls were purified before entering Heaven.

"This is a reflection of the longing for holiness," the voice declared, filled with compassion and clarity. "Yet my grace and my Son's sacrifice are sufficient. The work of purification is not bound to this realm, but to my Spirit and my truth."

Peter's gaze turned to the souls within this vision of Purgatory. They bore expressions of both hope and sorrow, their forms appearing refined by an invisible fire. The belief was that they were being cleansed of imperfections, preparing to enter the presence of the Creator.

"The desire to be pure before me is not misplaced," the voice said. "But the work of cleansing is accomplished through the blood of the Lamb, not through human striving or an intermediate state."

The vision shifted to the origins of this belief. Peter saw how the concept of Purgatory arose from humanity's awareness of their imperfection and their longing for a deeper communion with the Creator. It was a response to the tension between the holiness of Heaven and the lingering effects of sin.

"Humanity understands the weight of sin," the voice explained. "But they underestimate the power of my grace. My

Son's sacrifice is complete, and through Him, there is no condemnation for those who are in Christ Jesus."

Peter was shown the sufficiency of the Messiah's work. He saw the cross, where the weight of sin and guilt was borne by the Lamb. The blood of the Messiah was poured out, cleansing those who believed and granting them direct access to the Creator.

"It is finished," the voice declared. "The price has been paid in full. Those who are mine are washed clean, not by fire but by grace, not through striving but through faith."

The vision turned to the life of the believer on earth. Peter saw how the Spirit worked within the faithful, sanctifying them and conforming them to the image of the Messiah. This process, though not without struggle, was empowered by the Creator's presence and love.

"Sanctification is the work of my Spirit," the voice said. "It begins in life, not after death. Those who walk with me are refined by my truth, prepared for eternity through their daily communion with me."

Peter's attention was drawn to the hope of the resurrection. He saw the faithful rising in glory, their imperfections transformed in an instant. They were made perfect, their bodies and souls united in the fullness of the Creator's redemption.

"This is the final transformation," the voice declared. "In the twinkling of an eye, the corruptible is clothed with incorruptibility, and the mortal with immortality. There is no delay, for my work is complete in them through the power of my Son."

Peter was shown how the belief in Purgatory, though well-intentioned, often obscured the truth of the Gospel. He saw individuals weighed down by fear, believing that their entrance into Heaven depended on their own merit or on the prayers of others.

"Fear has no place in my perfect love," the voice said. "I have not given my children a spirit of fear, but of power, love, and a sound mind. My salvation is not partial but complete, given freely to all who believe."

The vision expanded to reveal the Creator's desire for humanity to trust fully in His grace. Peter saw the faithful living with assurance, their hope anchored in the Messiah's finished work. They did not strive to earn purification but rested in the knowledge that the Lamb had already accomplished all that was needed.

"Come boldly to my throne of grace," the voice said, filled with love. "There is no barrier, no delay. Through my Son, you are welcomed into my presence."

As the vision concluded, Peter was reminded of the Creator's heart for His people. The belief in Purgatory was born from a yearning for holiness, yet it was unnecessary in light of the Gospel's power. The Spirit worked within the faithful during their earthly lives, preparing them for the eternal joy of Heaven.

"My grace is sufficient," the voice declared. "Trust in me, and you will find rest. There is no need for an intermediate state, for my Son has opened the way to life everlasting."

When Peter returned from the vision, his heart was filled with both compassion and urgency. He gathered the faithful and spoke of what he had seen, his voice steady yet filled with grace.

"The work of purification is accomplished through the blood of the Lamb," Peter proclaimed. "There is no need for fear or striving, for His sacrifice is sufficient. Walk in faith, trusting in His grace, and live in the assurance of His love. For those who are in Christ, Heaven awaits without delay."

Peter's testimony stirred his listeners deeply. Some wept with relief, freed from the burden of uncertainty about their salvation. Others resolved to share the truth of the Messiah's complete work with those who clung to the belief in Purgatory.

Through his words, Peter emphasized the sufficiency of the Gospel and the joy of living in its freedom. The Creator's plan was not one of delay but of immediate communion, where faith in the Messiah brought complete restoration.

And as Peter continued to proclaim the vision, he prayed that all who heard would rest in the finished work of the Lamb, walking in the light of His grace and preparing their hearts for the eternal joy of dwelling with the Creator forever.

Chapter 40
Limbo

The vision opened with a realm suspended in stillness, a place neither of torment nor of joy. It was a state of waiting, where souls lingered in uncertainty. Peter stood at its edge, his heart heavy with questions about this concept of Limbo—a place imagined for those caught between salvation and separation from the Creator.

"This is a construct of human understanding," the voice declared, gentle yet resolute. "It reflects the yearning for answers, but my truth is not found in ambiguity. My justice is perfect, my mercy unending, and my plan complete."

Peter's gaze turned to the souls in this imagined realm. They appeared neither lost in despair nor radiant with joy, their state marked by a longing for something beyond. This belief, often associated with unbaptized infants or those who had lived without knowledge of the Creator, was an attempt to reconcile the tension between divine justice and mercy.

"The heart seeks to explain what it cannot grasp," the voice said. "Yet my ways are higher, and my grace surpasses all understanding. There is no Limbo, for my plan leaves no soul forgotten or forsaken."

The vision shifted to reveal the origins of this belief. Peter saw the early church wrestling with questions about the fate of those who had not heard the Gospel or who had died before receiving baptism. Limbo arose as an attempt to provide hope, yet it was rooted in uncertainty rather than the assurance of the Creator's promises.

"My justice is not incomplete," the voice explained. "I am not bound by human rituals or limitations. I see the heart, and my mercy reaches even the farthest corners."

Peter was shown the sufficiency of the Creator's grace. He saw the Messiah, His arms open to receive all who came to Him, regardless of their circumstances. The Lamb's sacrifice was not limited by human understanding but extended to all who sought the Creator, even in ways unseen by others.

"My Son's blood covers every sin," the voice declared. "To those who are mine, there is no barrier, no ambiguity. I call each soul to myself, and I am faithful to complete the work I have begun in them."

The vision turned to the fate of infants and others who had no opportunity to respond to the Gospel in life. Peter saw them in the arms of the Creator, their innocence embraced by His love. The voice spoke with deep compassion:

"I am the God of the living and the dead. My mercy is sufficient for these, and they rest in my care. Do not fear for them, for they are mine, and I will not lose one that has been entrusted to me."

Peter was shown how the Creator's justice and mercy worked in perfect harmony. He saw the balance between accountability and grace, each soul judged not by human standards but by the Creator's infinite wisdom and love.

"There is no Limbo," the voice said. "There is only life or separation, communion with me or rejection of my light. I desire that none should perish, and my call reaches all who have ears to hear."

As the vision concluded, Peter was reminded of the importance of trusting the Creator's plan. The concept of Limbo, while born of compassion, fell short of the truth revealed in the Gospel. The Creator's justice was complete, His mercy boundless, and His love for humanity unending.

"My truth does not dwell in uncertainty," the voice declared. "Trust in me, for I am the author and finisher of faith. I leave no soul unseen, no heart untouched by my call."

When Peter returned from the vision, his heart was filled with both clarity and comfort. He gathered the faithful and spoke of what he had seen, his voice steady yet filled with compassion.

"Limbo is not the plan of the Creator," Peter proclaimed. "His justice and mercy are complete, and His love reaches all who seek Him. Rest in His promises, and trust in His grace, for no soul is forgotten, no life beyond His care."

Peter's testimony stirred his listeners deeply. Some found solace in the assurance that the Creator's love extended to all, even those for whom answers seemed elusive. Others resolved to live more boldly in their faith, sharing the Gospel with those who had not yet heard.

Through his words, Peter emphasized the perfection of the Creator's justice and mercy. The Gospel left no room for uncertainty, only the assurance that every soul was known and loved by the One who created them.

And as Peter continued to proclaim the vision, he prayed that all who heard would rest in the certainty of the Creator's plan, trusting in His perfect justice and infinite mercy as they walked the path of faith toward eternal life.

Chapter 41
Predestination

The vision began in a vast expanse of light and shadow, where the past, present, and future wove together like an intricate tapestry. Peter stood at the edge of this divine mystery, his spirit humbled by the enormity of what lay before him. This was the doctrine of predestination—the belief that humanity's destiny is foreordained by the Creator's sovereign will.

"This is my plan," the voice declared, resonant with authority and love. "I know the end from the beginning. Yet my foreknowledge does not negate humanity's choice, for love must be freely given."

Peter's gaze turned to the tapestry, where threads of every human life were woven with purpose and intention. Each thread was unique, its pattern determined by the Creator's wisdom. Yet the hands that wove the tapestry allowed space for the choices of the souls it represented, shaping their destinies within the bounds of divine sovereignty.

"I am the Alpha and the Omega," the voice said. "I hold all things in my hands, yet I call each soul to choose life, to walk in my ways, and to find their place in my eternal plan."

The vision shifted to reveal the tension between divine predestination and human free will. Peter saw individuals standing at crossroads, their choices shaping their lives and destinies. Yet he also saw the hand of the Creator, guiding, sustaining, and working all things together for good.

"Predestination does not erase choice," the voice explained. "It ensures that my purposes are fulfilled, even through the decisions of my creation. I am sovereign, yet I honor the freedom I have given."

Peter was shown the role of the Messiah in predestination. He saw the Lamb, chosen before the foundation of the world, bearing the sins of humanity and opening the way for all to enter into the Creator's plan.

"My Son is the cornerstone of predestination," the voice declared. "Through Him, I have predestined a people for myself, chosen not by merit but by grace, that they might reflect my glory and share in my eternal life."

The vision turned to the faithful, those who had responded to the Creator's call. Peter saw their lives marked by trust, perseverance, and the assurance that they were held in the Creator's hands.

"They are my elect," the voice said, tender and resolute. "I have called them, justified them, and glorified them. None can snatch them from my hand, for my plan is unshakable, and my love is eternal."

Peter's gaze shifted to those who rejected the Creator's call. He saw their paths marked by rebellion and self-will, their choices leading them away from the light. Yet even here, the Creator's sorrow was evident, His desire that none should perish shining through the vision.

"I take no pleasure in the death of the wicked," the voice said. "My call is universal, my mercy unending. Yet love cannot be compelled, and their choice determines their destiny."

The vision expanded to reveal the complexity of predestination in human understanding. Peter saw theologians and believers wrestling with the doctrine, some finding assurance in the Creator's sovereignty, others struggling with its implications for human freedom and responsibility.

"This is a mystery," the voice said. "My ways are higher than your ways, my thoughts higher than your thoughts. Trust in my goodness, for I work all things according to the counsel of my will."

As the vision concluded, Peter was reminded of the Creator's ultimate purpose in predestination: to bring glory to His name and to draw humanity into a relationship with Him. The tension between sovereignty and free will was not a contradiction but a reflection of the Creator's infinite wisdom and love.

"My plan is perfect," the voice declared. "I have predestined my people to be conformed to the image of my Son, that they might walk in my light and share in my joy forever."

When Peter returned from the vision, his heart was filled with reverence and hope. Predestination was not a concept to fear but a truth to embrace, grounded in the Creator's love and sovereignty.

He gathered the faithful and spoke of what he had seen, his voice steady yet filled with awe.

"Predestination is the work of the Creator," Peter proclaimed. "It is His plan to draw all who believe into His eternal purpose. Trust in His sovereignty, walk in His light, and know that your destiny is secure in Him. His love is unshakable, His call unending—respond to it and live."

Peter's testimony stirred his listeners deeply. Some found comfort in the assurance of being held within the Creator's plan, while others reflected on the weight of their choices and the call to walk in faith.

Through his words, Peter emphasized the harmony between divine sovereignty and human responsibility. Predestination was not a denial of free will but a testament to the Creator's ability to work through every choice, bringing His purposes to fulfillment.

And as Peter continued to proclaim the vision, he prayed that all who heard would rest in the knowledge of the Creator's perfect plan, walking in trust and obedience as they embraced their place in His eternal design.

Chapter 42
The Apocalypse in Popular Culture

The vision began with a panorama of human creativity, spanning centuries and continents. Peter stood at the intersection of art, literature, music, and film, each medium echoing humanity's fascination with the Apocalypse. This was a realm where the divine revelation of the end times had been interpreted, reimagined, and retold countless times, weaving itself into the fabric of popular culture.

"This is how my message has been refracted through human imagination," the voice declared, resonant with both curiosity and solemnity. "Some reflect truth, others distort it, yet all reveal humanity's enduring longing to understand what lies beyond the veil of time."

Peter's gaze turned to ancient manuscripts and early artworks inspired by the Apocalypse. He saw illuminated texts depicting the triumph of the Lamb, frescoes portraying the final judgment, and hymns that gave voice to the hope of eternal life. These creations were rooted in reverence, their intent to inspire faith and awe.

"Through these works," the voice said, "my message was preserved and shared. They reflect the yearning for hope and the assurance of my promises."

The vision shifted to more modern interpretations. Peter saw novels and films that sought to dramatize the Apocalypse, often blending biblical themes with speculative storytelling. He witnessed grand battles between good and evil, vivid depictions of divine wrath, and stories that sought to explore humanity's resilience in the face of ultimate destruction.

"Here, creativity seeks to grapple with my revelation," the voice explained. "Yet in the pursuit of spectacle, my truth is sometimes overshadowed. What is meant to inspire repentance and faith becomes a tale of fear and entertainment."

Peter observed how the Apocalypse had been used as a tool for warning and persuasion. He saw street preachers, artists, and filmmakers who used vivid imagery of judgment to stir people toward faith. Yet he also saw how some wielded the Apocalypse as a weapon of fear, distorting its message of hope and redemption.

"My word is not a weapon of terror," the voice declared. "It is a call to life, a beacon of hope for the faithful. Let those who speak of my coming do so with love and truth, not with manipulation or despair."

The vision turned to the enduring themes of the Apocalypse in popular culture. Peter saw humanity's fascination with the battle between good and evil, the hope of justice, and the promise of renewal. These elements resonated deeply, transcending time and culture, reflecting the eternal truths woven into the Creator's plan.

"They do not always name me," the voice said, "yet their hearts echo my truth. The longing for justice, the hope for renewal, the belief in the triumph of good—these are the seeds of my word, planted in every soul."

Peter was shown the dangers of misrepresentation. He saw works that trivialized the Apocalypse, reducing it to mere entertainment, and others that distorted its message for personal or political gain. These misinterpretations often led to confusion, fear, or cynicism, turning hearts away from the Creator's love.

"Guard my truth," the voice said. "Do not let it be diluted or misused. Speak of the Apocalypse as it was revealed—solemn, yes, but filled with hope, for it is the culmination of my plan to dwell with my people forever."

The vision revealed the potential of popular culture to serve as a bridge to the Gospel. Peter saw stories and songs that opened doors for conversations about faith, prompting seekers to explore the Creator's word. Even when imperfect, these works had the power to plant seeds of curiosity and longing.

"I use all things for my purpose," the voice declared. "Even in the flawed and fragmented, my Spirit moves, calling hearts to me. Let my people be wise, using these opportunities to share my truth."

As the vision concluded, Peter was reminded of the responsibility of the faithful to engage with popular culture thoughtfully. He saw the importance of discernment, of separating truth from distortion, and of using the Apocalypse as a means to point others to the Creator's love and redemption.

"Be my witnesses," the voice said. "Speak of my coming with grace and truth. Let your lives reflect the hope of my promises, so that others may see and believe."

When Peter returned from the vision, his heart was filled with both caution and hope. The Apocalypse in popular culture was a powerful force, capable of inspiring faith or spreading fear, depending on how it was approached.

He gathered the faithful and spoke of what he had seen, his voice steady yet filled with conviction.

"The Apocalypse is not a story to entertain but a truth to transform," Peter proclaimed. "Engage with popular culture wisely, using it as a bridge to share the Gospel. Speak of the Lamb and His victory, and let your words and actions reflect the hope of His coming."

Peter's testimony stirred his listeners deeply. Some reflected on how they had consumed or shared stories of the Apocalypse, resolving to approach these narratives with greater discernment. Others felt inspired to create works of art and storytelling that honored the Creator's truth and drew others to His light.

Through his words, Peter emphasized the power of popular culture to influence hearts and minds. The Apocalypse, when shared faithfully, was not merely a tale of judgment but a message of hope and renewal for all who turned to the Creator.

And as Peter continued to proclaim the vision, he prayed that all who heard would engage with popular culture as ambassadors of the Gospel, using every opportunity to share the hope of the Lamb's victory and the joy of the Creator's eternal kingdom.

Chapter 43
The Meaning of the Apocalypse

The vision began with a sweeping panorama of creation, from the first spark of existence to the culmination of the Creator's plan. Peter stood amidst this grand narrative, his spirit attuned to the profound significance of the Apocalypse. It was not merely an end but a revelation—a divine unveiling of the Creator's purpose for humanity and all things.

"This is my story," the voice declared, resonant with both authority and tenderness. "The Apocalypse is not destruction for its own sake but the fulfillment of my promise to make all things new."

Peter's gaze turned to the cycles of history, where humanity's choices had shaped the world's destiny. He saw moments of faith and rebellion, triumph and tragedy. The Apocalypse, as revealed to him, was the resolution of these cycles—a time when justice would be served, mercy extended, and creation restored.

"It is the climax of the story I have written," the voice said. "It is not merely the end of days but the beginning of eternity, where my people dwell with me forever."

The vision shifted to the Apocalypse as a revelation of the Creator's character. Peter saw the Creator's justice in the judgment of sin, His mercy in the call to repentance, and His love in the promise of redemption. Each aspect of the Apocalypse reflected a facet of the Creator's nature, drawing humanity closer to understanding His heart.

"My ways are not hidden," the voice explained. "Through the Apocalypse, I reveal my holiness, my patience, and my desire for all to come to life. It is a call to see me as I am, to trust in my plan, and to walk in my light."

Peter was shown the Apocalypse as a message of hope for the faithful. He saw the promises of the Messiah fulfilled—the defeat of evil, the resurrection of the dead, and the establishment of the eternal kingdom. For those who believed, the Apocalypse was not a message of fear but of victory and assurance.

"To my people, the Apocalypse is not a warning but a promise," the voice declared. "It is the triumph of the Lamb, the restoration of all that was lost, and the fulfillment of every longing."

The vision turned to the universal relevance of the Apocalypse. Peter saw how its themes resonated with every generation, addressing humanity's deepest fears and hopes. The longing for justice, the need for renewal, and the promise of a better future were woven into the fabric of the Apocalypse, making it a message for all people.

"My word is eternal," the voice said. "Though the times and cultures change, the truth of the Apocalypse endures. It speaks to every heart, calling them to seek me and to find their place in my plan."

Peter's spirit was drawn to the responsibility of the faithful to share the meaning of the Apocalypse. He saw the importance of living as witnesses to its truth, not merely in words but in actions that reflected the Creator's love and justice.

"Let my people be light in the darkness," the voice declared. "Through their lives, let the world see the hope of my coming and the joy of my presence. The meaning of the Apocalypse is not only in what is to come but in how you live today."

The vision revealed the Creator's ultimate purpose in the Apocalypse: to dwell with His people forever. Peter saw the New Jerusalem descending, its gates open to all who had walked in faith. The Creator's presence filled the city, and His light banished all darkness.

"This is my desire," the voice said, filled with love. "To be with my people, to wipe away every tear, to restore what was broken, and to make all things new. This is the meaning of the Apocalypse—a revelation of my eternal love."

As the vision concluded, Peter was reminded of the hope and urgency of the Apocalypse. It was not merely a distant event but a present reality, calling humanity to live with purpose, faith, and expectation.

"The Apocalypse is my promise," the voice declared. "It is my call to you and to all who hear. Live in its light, share its hope, and prepare for the day when my kingdom comes in fullness."

When Peter returned from the vision, his heart was filled with reverence and determination. The meaning of the Apocalypse was not to instill fear but to inspire faith, offering hope to a world in need of redemption.

He gathered the faithful and spoke of what he had seen, his voice steady yet filled with passion.

"The Apocalypse is the Creator's revelation," Peter proclaimed. "It is the fulfillment of His plan, the triumph of His justice, and the promise of His love. Live as those who believe, share the hope of His coming, and walk in the light of His truth. For the day is near when all will be made new."

Peter's testimony stirred his listeners deeply. Some found renewed purpose in their faith, resolving to live in light of the Apocalypse's promise. Others felt the urgency to share its message, reaching out to those who had yet to hear of the Creator's love.

Through his words, Peter emphasized the transformative power of the Apocalypse. It was not an end but a beginning, a call to live with hope and expectation as the Creator's plan unfolded.

And as Peter continued to proclaim the vision, he prayed that all who heard would embrace the meaning of the Apocalypse, living as witnesses to the Creator's love and preparing their hearts for the day when His eternal kingdom would be fully realized.

Chapter 44
Hope in Difficult Times

The vision unfolded in a world cloaked in shadow, where trials and tribulations pressed heavily upon the hearts of humanity. Peter stood amidst scenes of suffering—wars that ravaged lands, poverty that stripped dignity, and grief that weighed on souls. Yet even in this darkness, glimmers of light pierced through, symbols of hope that refused to be extinguished.

"This is the endurance of my people," the voice declared, resonant with both strength and compassion. "Though the world is fraught with trouble, my promises stand firm. I am the anchor of their hope, unshaken and eternal."

Peter's gaze turned to the faithful, scattered across the earth. He saw their struggles, moments of doubt, and the tears shed in silence. Yet he also saw their perseverance, their hands clasped in prayer, and their hearts clinging to the promises of the Creator.

"My hope is not fragile," the voice said. "It is a fortress in the storm, a light that guides through the deepest valley. My people are not alone, for I am with them always."

The vision shifted to reveal the source of hope in difficult times: the Creator's unchanging nature. Peter saw the Lamb standing at the center of all things, His wounds a testimony to His victory. From Him flowed rivers of life, bringing renewal to those who drank deeply of His grace.

"My hope is not wishful thinking," the voice declared. "It is the certainty of my love, the assurance of my promises, and the power of my presence. Those who trust in me will not be put to shame."

Peter was shown how hope sustained the faithful throughout history. He saw Abraham trusting in the promise of a child, even when it seemed impossible. He witnessed the Israelites clinging to the hope of deliverance as they wandered in the wilderness. He saw the early church, steadfast in the face of persecution, their eyes fixed on the eternal kingdom.

"My people have always faced trials," the voice explained. "Yet through every storm, I have been their refuge. My hope is not bound by circumstances but rooted in my faithfulness."

The vision turned to the role of the community in fostering hope. Peter saw believers gathering together, sharing their burdens, and encouraging one another. Their unity became a beacon of light in the darkness, a testament to the Creator's love.

"Bear one another's burdens," the voice said. "Through your love for one another, the world will see my presence among you. Hope grows when it is shared, and joy is multiplied when my people walk together in faith."

Peter's spirit was drawn to the promises of the Apocalypse, where ultimate hope resided. He saw the faithful entering the New Jerusalem, their sorrows turned to joy, their tears wiped away by the hand of the Creator. The trials of the present were eclipsed by the glory of the eternal.

"This is the hope that does not fade," the voice declared. "The promise of my kingdom, where justice reigns and love abounds. Let this hope anchor your souls, for it is the assurance of things unseen."

The vision revealed practical ways the faithful could live out hope in difficult times. Peter saw acts of kindness—a cup of water given in love, a word of encouragement spoken in despair, a hand extended to the weary. These small gestures became lifelines, drawing others toward the Creator's light.

"Hope is not passive," the voice said. "It is active, a force that moves hearts and changes lives. Be my hands and feet, bringing hope to a hurting world."

As the vision concluded, Peter was reminded of the Creator's call to perseverance. Hope was not the absence of difficulty but the presence of trust in the One who held all things.

"Do not grow weary," the voice said. "For in due season, you will reap if you do not lose heart. My grace is sufficient for every trial, and my strength is made perfect in your weakness."

When Peter returned from the vision, his heart was filled with both compassion and determination. Hope in difficult times was not merely an ideal but a reality rooted in the Creator's promises.

He gathered the faithful and spoke of what he had seen, his voice steady yet filled with encouragement.

"Hope is the anchor of our souls," Peter proclaimed. "It is not bound by the trials we face but rests in the faithfulness of the Creator. Trust in His promises, encourage one another, and live as those who carry His light. For the darkness cannot overcome the hope we have in Him."

Peter's testimony stirred his listeners deeply. Some found strength to face their struggles, their hearts renewed by the assurance of the Creator's love. Others resolved to be agents of hope, reaching out to those in need with compassion and faith.

Through his words, Peter emphasized the power of hope to sustain, to heal, and to transform. It was not an abstract concept but a tangible reality, a gift from the Creator that carried His people through the storms of life.

And as Peter continued to proclaim the vision, he prayed that all who heard would embrace the hope of the Creator, living as witnesses to His faithfulness and pointing others to the joy of His eternal promises.

Chapter 45
The Importance of Faith

The vision unfolded in a vast expanse where the unseen was more tangible than the visible. Peter stood among countless figures who walked with certainty, their steps guided not by what they could see but by the promises they believed. Faith was the substance of their journey, the bridge between humanity and the Creator's eternal purposes.

"This is the foundation of my people," the voice declared, filled with strength and gentleness. "Faith is the key that unlocks the fullness of my promises. It is trust in what cannot be seen but is eternally true."

Peter's gaze turned to the heroes of faith who had walked before him. He saw Abraham, leaving his homeland for a place he had never seen, trusting in the Creator's word. He saw Moses, standing before the Red Sea, his faith parting the waters. He saw David, facing Goliath with nothing but a sling and his trust in the Almighty.

"These are my faithful ones," the voice said. "They did not see the outcome, yet they believed. Through their faith, my power was made manifest, and my will accomplished."

The vision shifted to the life of the Messiah, where faith was embodied perfectly. Peter saw the Messiah in the garden, His prayers marked by submission and trust. He saw Him on the cross, His faith unwavering even in the face of death. Through His faith, humanity was reconciled to the Creator, and the path to salvation was opened.

"My Son is the author and finisher of faith," the voice declared. "Through Him, you see what faith can accomplish. In Him, your faith finds its anchor, its assurance, and its fulfillment."

Peter was shown the daily lives of the faithful, where faith was not merely a moment but a continual journey. He saw individuals trusting in the Creator's provision during scarcity, believing in healing amidst sickness, and holding onto hope in the face of despair.

"Faith is not the absence of struggle," the voice explained. "It is the presence of trust in the midst of it. It is the assurance that I am with you, that my promises are true, and that my plans are good."

The vision turned to the challenges to faith. Peter saw doubts creeping into hearts, storms that tested convictions, and voices that sought to undermine trust in the Creator. Yet he also saw the Spirit moving within the faithful, strengthening their resolve and reminding them of the truth.

"Faith is a shield," the voice said. "It extinguishes the fiery darts of the enemy. Though trials come, my Spirit sustains, and my word assures. Hold fast to your faith, for it is your victory."

Peter's spirit was drawn to the community of believers, where faith was nurtured and strengthened. He saw them gathering in worship, sharing testimonies of the Creator's faithfulness, and encouraging one another to persevere.

"Faith grows in community," the voice declared. "As iron sharpens iron, so my people strengthen one another. Together, they are a light to the world, a city on a hill that cannot be hidden."

The vision revealed the eternal significance of faith. Peter saw the faithful standing before the Creator, their lives a testament to their trust. Their faith had shaped their actions, their choices, and their legacy. They had walked by faith, not by sight, and now entered the joy of their Lord.

"Without faith, it is impossible to please me," the voice said. "Yet to those who believe, all things are possible. Their faith has saved them, and their reward is eternal life with me."

As the vision concluded, Peter was reminded of the call to live by faith. It was not a passive belief but an active trust that shaped every aspect of life. Faith was the foundation of hope, the catalyst for love, and the pathway to the Creator's promises.

"Walk by faith," the voice said. "Not by what you see, but by what you know to be true in me. Faith will sustain you, guide you, and lead you home."

When Peter returned from the vision, his heart was filled with conviction and encouragement. The importance of faith was not merely a theological concept but a daily reality, a lifeline to the Creator's presence and power.

He gathered the faithful and spoke of what he had seen, his voice steady yet filled with passion.

"Faith is the foundation of our lives," Peter proclaimed. "It is trust in the Creator's promises, the assurance of His presence, and the key to His eternal kingdom. Hold fast to your faith, encourage one another, and live as those who believe, for the righteous shall live by faith."

Peter's testimony stirred his listeners deeply. Some found renewed strength to face their trials, their faith rekindled by the reminder of the Creator's faithfulness. Others resolved to encourage those struggling with doubt, becoming beacons of hope within their community.

Through his words, Peter emphasized the transformative power of faith. It was not an abstract idea but a living force that connected humanity to the Creator, shaping their lives and destinies.

And as Peter continued to proclaim the vision, he prayed that all who heard would walk by faith, trusting in the Creator's promises and living as witnesses to His love, until the day they stood before Him in the fullness of His glory.

Chapter 46
Love for Others

The vision began in a radiant garden, filled with life and color, where every living thing seemed to thrive in harmony. Peter stood in awe as he observed countless acts of selfless care and kindness. In this place, love for others was the essence that bound everything together, a reflection of the Creator's eternal nature.

"This is my commandment," the voice declared, filled with tenderness and authority. "That you love one another as I have loved you. In this, the world will see me, and my kingdom will be revealed."

Peter's gaze turned to the life of the Messiah, the perfect embodiment of love. He saw Him healing the sick, feeding the hungry, and comforting the brokenhearted. He witnessed the Messiah washing the feet of His disciples, His humility a profound lesson in serving others.

"This is love in action," the voice explained. "Not in words alone, but in deeds that reflect my heart. My Son's life was given, not taken. Through Him, you see the measure of true love: to lay down your life for others."

The vision shifted to reveal the struggles of humanity, where selfishness and division often overshadowed love. Peter saw families torn apart by conflict, communities fractured by prejudice, and nations divided by greed and power. Yet amidst the darkness, acts of love shone like beacons—small yet powerful gestures that brought healing and reconciliation.

"Love is the greatest commandment," the voice declared. "It overcomes hatred, heals wounds, and binds together what sin has torn apart. Through love, my people become my witnesses, a light to the world."

Peter was shown how love for others was essential to living out faith. He saw believers sharing their resources with those in need, welcoming strangers into their homes, and forgiving those who had wronged them. These acts of love were not mere obligations but joyful expressions of the Creator's presence within them.

"Faith without love is nothing," the voice said. "Though you speak with the tongues of angels or possess all knowledge, without love, you are but a clanging cymbal. Let your love for others be the proof of your faith in me."

The vision turned to the transformative power of love. Peter saw relationships restored, communities rebuilt, and lives changed through acts of kindness and compassion. Love was not weak but strong, breaking down barriers and bridging divides.

"Love conquers all," the voice declared. "It is the greatest force in the universe, for it flows from my very being. My love has no bounds, and through it, all things are made new."

Peter's spirit was drawn to the command to love even enemies. He saw individuals reaching out to those who had harmed them, offering forgiveness and seeking peace. This love, though costly, bore witness to the Creator's mercy and grace.

"To love those who love you is easy," the voice said. "But to love your enemies, to bless those who curse you—this is the love that reflects my heart. In this, you show the world that you are my children."

The vision expanded to reveal the eternal significance of love. Peter saw the faithful standing before the Creator, their lives marked by their love for others. They were welcomed into the eternal kingdom, where love was the language of Heaven and the essence of every action.

"This is the greatest commandment," the voice declared. "To love me with all your heart, soul, and mind, and to love your neighbor as yourself. In this, all the law and the prophets are fulfilled."

As the vision concluded, Peter was reminded of the urgency of living a life of love. It was not merely a virtue but a command, the foundation of the Creator's kingdom on earth and in eternity.

"Love one another as I have loved you," the voice said. "In this, my glory is revealed, and my kingdom comes. Let your love be genuine, patient, and enduring, for it reflects my presence in you."

When Peter returned from the vision, his heart was filled with compassion and determination. Love for others was not an option but the essence of faith, a call to reflect the Creator's character in every aspect of life.

He gathered the faithful and spoke of what he had seen, his voice steady yet filled with warmth.

"Love is the greatest commandment," Peter proclaimed. "Through it, the Creator's presence is made known, and His kingdom revealed. Let us love one another with humility and sincerity, serving as the Messiah served, forgiving as He forgave, and living as He lived. For in love, we find the fulfillment of His will."

Peter's testimony stirred his listeners deeply. Some resolved to mend broken relationships, reaching out with forgiveness and compassion. Others felt compelled to serve their communities, bringing the Creator's love to those in need.

Through his words, Peter emphasized the transformative and eternal power of love. It was not a passive sentiment but an active force that shaped lives, healed wounds, and built the Creator's kingdom on earth.

And as Peter continued to proclaim the vision, he prayed that all who heard would embrace the call to love, living as vessels of the Creator's compassion and light until the day they stood together in the eternal kingdom, where love reigns forever.

Chapter 47
The Pursuit of Justice

The vision opened with a scene of a world deeply divided, where injustice reigned in many forms. Peter stood amidst towering structures of power built on the backs of the oppressed. He saw wealth hoarded by a few while many suffered in poverty, and courts corrupted, their judgments favoring the strong over the weak. Yet in the midst of this darkness, rays of light broke through—the acts of those who pursued justice, driven by the Creator's call.

"This is my command," the voice declared, filled with both righteous indignation and profound love. "Let justice roll down like waters, and righteousness like a mighty stream. For I am the God of justice, and my people must walk in my ways."

Peter's gaze was drawn to the prophets of old, who stood as voices of truth in a world rife with inequity. He saw Amos crying out against the exploitation of the poor, Isaiah calling for the breaking of every yoke, and Micah proclaiming the Creator's requirement to act justly, love mercy, and walk humbly.

"These are my messengers," the voice said. "Through them, I revealed my heart for the oppressed, my anger at injustice, and my promise to bring restoration. Justice is not an option for my people—it is their calling."

The vision shifted to the life of the Messiah, where justice and mercy walked hand in hand. Peter saw Him healing the sick, welcoming the outcast, and challenging the hypocrisy of the powerful. The Messiah's actions were a testament to the Creator's justice, not merely punishing the wicked but uplifting the downtrodden and restoring dignity to the broken.

"My Son is the embodiment of justice," the voice declared. "Through Him, I established a kingdom where the last shall be first, and the least shall be greatest. Let my people follow His example, seeking justice not for themselves but for others."

Peter was shown the cost of pursuing justice. He saw individuals standing against corruption and oppression, their voices silenced by violence and persecution. Yet he also saw their sacrifices bear fruit, inspiring others to continue the fight for righteousness.

"Justice is not without cost," the voice said. "But blessed are those who hunger and thirst for righteousness, for they shall be satisfied. My Spirit sustains those who walk in my ways, even in the face of great opposition."

The vision turned to the systems and structures that perpetuated injustice. Peter saw economies built on exploitation, laws that marginalized the vulnerable, and leaders who wielded power without accountability. Yet he also saw the faithful working to dismantle these systems, replacing them with structures rooted in fairness, compassion, and truth.

"My justice is not limited to individuals," the voice explained. "It extends to nations, communities, and systems. Let my people be agents of change, transforming the world to reflect my kingdom."

Peter's spirit was drawn to the promise of ultimate justice. He saw the throne of the Creator, where every wrong was made right, every tear wiped away, and every act of injustice brought to account. The faithful stood in the light, their efforts in pursuing justice honored, while the oppressors faced the consequences of their actions.

"My justice is perfect," the voice said. "Though it may seem delayed, it is never denied. Trust in me, for I will bring justice to the nations, and my righteousness will shine like the dawn."

The vision revealed practical ways the faithful could pursue justice in their daily lives. Peter saw acts of advocacy for the voiceless, generosity toward the needy, and courage in confronting wrongdoing. Each action, though small, contributed to the greater work of building the Creator's kingdom.

"Justice begins with love," the voice declared. "It is not born of anger or pride but of compassion and humility. Let your actions flow from my heart, and you will reflect my justice in the world."

As the vision concluded, Peter was reminded of the importance of perseverance in the pursuit of justice. Though the journey was fraught with challenges, the Creator's promise of restoration was sure.

"Do not grow weary in doing good," the voice said. "For in due time, you will reap a harvest if you do not give up. Let justice and righteousness guide your steps, and you will walk in my light."

When Peter returned from the vision, his heart burned with both righteous anger and hope. The pursuit of justice was not merely an ideal but a mandate, a reflection of the Creator's character and kingdom.

He gathered the faithful and spoke of what he had seen, his voice steady yet charged with conviction.

"Justice is the will of the Creator," Peter proclaimed. "It is not enough to believe—we must act, lifting the oppressed, defending the vulnerable, and confronting injustice wherever it is found. Walk in His ways, for His justice is perfect, and His kingdom is near."

Peter's testimony stirred his listeners deeply. Some resolved to confront the injustices in their own communities, while others found strength to continue their work in advocacy and service.

Through his words, Peter emphasized the Creator's call to action. Justice was not an abstract concept but a living command, one that required courage, sacrifice, and steadfast faith.

And as Peter continued to proclaim the vision, he prayed that all who heard would embrace the pursuit of justice, living as agents of the Creator's righteousness and preparing the way for the eternal kingdom, where justice and peace would reign forever.

Chapter 48
Forgiveness and Reconciliation

The vision began in a fractured landscape, where broken relationships left deep chasms between individuals, families, and communities. Peter stood at the edge of one such divide, feeling the weight of resentment, anger, and sorrow that kept hearts apart. Yet amidst this scene of separation, a light emerged—a figure stepping forward to offer a hand, bridging the gap with an act of forgiveness.

"This is my command," the voice declared, filled with both compassion and authority. "Forgive as I have forgiven you. Through forgiveness, you reveal my mercy, and through reconciliation, you proclaim my love."

Peter's gaze turned to the life of the Messiah, the ultimate example of forgiveness. He saw Him dining with sinners, healing those who had wronged others, and offering mercy to those condemned. On the cross, Peter witnessed the Messiah's words echo through the ages: "Father, forgive them, for they know not what they do."

"This is the heart of forgiveness," the voice said. "It is not earned but freely given, a gift that mirrors my grace. My Son bore the weight of sin so that all might be reconciled to me and to one another."

The vision shifted to humanity's struggle with forgiveness. Peter saw individuals clutching tightly to their pain, unable to release the bitterness that consumed them. He witnessed families torn apart by grudges, communities divided by prejudice, and nations unwilling to reconcile their past wounds.

"Unforgiveness is a chain," the voice declared. "It binds the soul and blinds the heart. Yet my Spirit offers freedom, breaking every chain through the power of my mercy."

Peter was shown the process of forgiveness, a journey that began with the heart's willingness to release the offense. He saw the Spirit moving within individuals, softening their hearts and giving them the strength to let go of their pain. This act of forgiveness, though difficult, brought healing not only to the forgiver but also to those who had wronged them.

"Forgiveness is not weakness," the voice said. "It is strength born of my love. When you forgive, you reflect my image, and my power is made perfect in your humility."

The vision turned to reconciliation, the fruit of forgiveness. Peter saw relationships restored, families reunited, and communities rebuilt. These acts of reconciliation were not superficial but profound, rooted in honesty, repentance, and the desire to heal.

"Reconciliation is my will," the voice declared. "It is the restoration of what was broken, the mending of what sin has torn apart. Through reconciliation, my kingdom is revealed on earth as it is in Heaven."

Peter's spirit was drawn to the cost of forgiveness and reconciliation. He saw individuals laying down their pride, acknowledging their own faults, and seeking to make amends. These acts required courage and humility, yet they bore witness to the Creator's transforming power.

"My forgiveness was not without cost," the voice said. "It was purchased by the blood of my Son. Likewise, your forgiveness may cost you pride, comfort, or control, but its reward is far greater—a heart set free and relationships made whole."

The vision revealed the eternal significance of forgiveness and reconciliation. Peter saw the faithful standing before the Creator, their lives marked by acts of mercy and love. The divisions of the world were no more, and all who had embraced forgiveness walked together in the light of the Lamb.

"In my kingdom, there is no division," the voice declared. "There is only unity, born of my love and sustained by my grace. Forgive, reconcile, and walk as one, for this is the path to eternal joy."

As the vision concluded, Peter was reminded of the urgency of forgiveness and reconciliation. They were not merely suggestions but commands, essential to living in the Creator's will and reflecting His nature to the world.

"Do not let the sun go down on your anger," the voice said. "Forgive quickly, love deeply, and seek peace with all. In this, you reveal my glory and prepare your hearts for my kingdom."

When Peter returned from the vision, his heart was filled with both conviction and hope. Forgiveness and reconciliation were not optional—they were the essence of the Creator's work in humanity.

He gathered the faithful and spoke of what he had seen, his voice steady yet filled with compassion.

"Forgiveness is the key to freedom," Peter proclaimed. "Reconciliation is the fruit of love. Let us forgive as we have been forgiven, and seek to mend what has been broken. In doing so, we proclaim the mercy of the Creator and walk in the light of His truth."

Peter's testimony stirred his listeners deeply. Some wept as they resolved to forgive those who had wronged them, while others felt called to seek reconciliation in relationships long neglected.

Through his words, Peter emphasized the transformative power of forgiveness and reconciliation. These acts were not easy, but they were necessary, bringing healing to individuals, families, and communities.

And as Peter continued to proclaim the vision, he prayed that all who heard would embrace the call to forgive and reconcile, living as agents of the Creator's love until the day they stood together in the eternal kingdom, united in the light of His

Chapter 49
Life in Community

The vision unfolded in a vibrant gathering of people, united in purpose and filled with joy. Peter stood amidst this harmonious assembly, where differences of culture, language, and background were embraced rather than dividing. Each person contributed something unique, and together they reflected the Creator's love and glory. This was life in community, the design and desire of the Creator for His people.

"This is my will," the voice declared, filled with warmth and wisdom. "That my people dwell together in unity. In community, you reflect my image, for I am not isolation but communion."

Peter's gaze turned to the early church, where believers gathered to share meals, worship, and their possessions. He saw their acts of generosity, where no one claimed anything as their own, and all needs were met. This community thrived not through uniformity but through shared faith, love, and purpose.

"They devoted themselves to fellowship and to the breaking of bread," the voice said. "This is the blueprint for my people. In their unity, they reveal my presence to the world."

The vision shifted to the Messiah's ministry, where community was central. Peter saw Him calling His disciples, teaching them not only as individuals but as a group bound together by a shared mission. He witnessed the Messiah dining with sinners, healing the marginalized, and bridging divides between people.

"My Son built His kingdom through relationships," the voice declared. "He called others to walk with Him, to bear one another's burdens, and to love as He loved. In this, He revealed my heart for community."

Peter was shown the challenges of living in community. He saw misunderstandings, conflicts, and selfishness threaten to divide people. Yet he also saw the Spirit moving within these gatherings, bringing reconciliation, patience, and humility. The act of living in community was not without struggle, but it was through these struggles that love was deepened and faith strengthened.

"Community is not without trials," the voice said. "But it is through these trials that my people grow. Bear with one another, forgive as I have forgiven you, and let my Spirit bind you together in perfect unity."

The vision turned to the role of community in supporting the faithful through hardship. Peter saw believers comforting the grieving, encouraging the weary, and celebrating victories together. In these acts, the Creator's love became tangible, a lifeline for those in need.

"Where two or three are gathered in my name, there I am with them," the voice declared. "In community, my presence is made manifest. Through your love for one another, the world will know that you are mine."

Peter's spirit was drawn to the importance of diversity within community. He saw people of different gifts, backgrounds, and perspectives coming together to build something greater than themselves. Each contribution, no matter how small, played a vital role in the Creator's plan.

"My body is one, though it has many parts," the voice said. "Each member is essential, and each gift is given for the good of all. Let no one consider themselves greater or lesser, for all are equal in my sight."

The vision revealed the eternal significance of life in community. Peter saw the faithful gathered in the New Jerusalem, their voices united in praise. There was no division, no isolation—only perfect communion with the Creator and one another. This eternal fellowship was the fulfillment of the Creator's desire for His people.

"This is my kingdom," the voice declared. "A community of love, where every tear is wiped away, and every heart is made whole. Live now as citizens of this kingdom, reflecting its unity and joy."

As the vision concluded, Peter was reminded of the responsibility to nurture and protect community. It was not merely a human construct but a divine calling, a reflection of the Creator's own nature.

"Do not forsake meeting together," the voice said. "Encourage one another, serve one another, and build each other up. In community, you fulfill my command to love, and you prepare your hearts for eternity."

When Peter returned from the vision, his heart was filled with gratitude and resolve. Life in community was not optional—it was essential, a living testament to the Creator's love and presence.

He gathered the faithful and spoke of what he had seen, his voice steady yet filled with warmth.

"Community is the Creator's design," Peter proclaimed. "It is where we find strength, purpose, and joy. Let us live as one body, bearing one another's burdens and rejoicing together in His grace. For in our unity, the world will see His glory, and in our love, His kingdom will come."

Peter's testimony stirred his listeners deeply. Some resolved to strengthen their relationships within the community, offering forgiveness and support where it was needed. Others felt called to reach out to those on the margins, inviting them into the fellowship of faith.

Through his words, Peter emphasized the transformative power of community. It was not merely a gathering but a reflection of the Creator's kingdom, where love, service, and unity reigned.

And as Peter continued to proclaim the vision, he prayed that all who heard would embrace life in community, living as ambassadors of the Creator's love and preparing their hearts for the eternal fellowship that awaited in His kingdom.

Chapter 50
Caring for Creation

The vision began with a breathtaking panorama of the earth, vibrant and alive. Peter stood amidst lush forests, cascading waterfalls, and fields teeming with life. Each element of creation seemed to sing in harmony, a testament to the Creator's craftsmanship. Yet, as the vision shifted, Peter saw scars upon the earth—polluted rivers, desolate landscapes, and creatures driven to extinction by human neglect.

"This is my creation," the voice declared, resonant with both joy and sorrow. "I formed it good and entrusted it to humanity's care. Yet they have forgotten their stewardship, choosing exploitation over protection."

Peter's gaze turned to the garden of Eden, where humanity's relationship with creation began. He saw Adam and Eve tending the garden, their hands nurturing the soil, their lives intertwined with the earth. This stewardship was not a burden but a calling, a reflection of the Creator's love for what He had made.

"I gave you dominion," the voice said, "not to destroy but to cultivate, to rule with wisdom and compassion, as I rule over you. Creation is my gift to you, and your care for it is an act of worship."

The vision shifted to the ways humanity had failed in this calling. Peter saw forests cleared without thought, oceans choked with waste, and the air thick with smoke. He witnessed the suffering of creatures and people alike, their lives diminished by greed and carelessness.

"Sin has marred my creation," the voice declared. "Yet my heart remains for it, and I call my people to restore what has been broken. Your care for the earth reflects your love for me, for what you do to my creation, you do to me."

Peter was shown the interconnectedness of creation, how every element depended on the others. He saw how neglect in one area led to suffering in another, and how small acts of care could ripple outward, bringing healing to the land and its inhabitants.

"Creation is not separate from you," the voice explained. "It is the stage upon which my story unfolds, and it groans with eager longing for the day of its renewal. Care for it, as you care for one another."

The vision turned to the faithful, who were called to lead in caring for creation. Peter saw believers planting trees, cleaning rivers, and advocating for policies that protected the earth. Their actions were acts of obedience and love, rooted in the Creator's command to steward His gift.

"My people are to be the light of the world," the voice said. "Let their care for creation be a testimony to my love and a reflection of my kingdom. Through their hands, I will bring restoration."

Peter's spirit was drawn to the promise of creation's redemption. He saw the New Heaven and New Earth, where the scars of sin were no more. The rivers ran pure, the trees bore fruit in every season, and all creatures lived in harmony.

"This is my promise," the voice declared. "I will renew what has been broken and restore what has been lost. Yet until that day, I call you to be stewards of hope, caretakers of what I have entrusted to you."

The vision revealed practical ways the faithful could care for creation. Peter saw families reducing waste, communities working together to protect natural resources, and individuals choosing to live simply, mindful of their impact on the earth.

"Small acts matter," the voice said. "Do not grow weary in doing good, for each act of care reflects my love and brings you closer to my heart. In your stewardship, my glory is revealed."

As the vision concluded, Peter was reminded of the sacredness of creation and humanity's responsibility to protect it.

Caring for the earth was not merely an environmental concern but a spiritual act, a reflection of the Creator's character and will.

"Honor me by honoring my creation," the voice said. "Protect it, restore it, and cherish it, for it is a testament to my love and a gift to all generations."

When Peter returned from the vision, his heart was filled with both reverence and resolve. Caring for creation was not a secondary concern but an integral part of living in obedience to the Creator.

He gathered the faithful and spoke of what he had seen, his voice steady yet filled with urgency.

"Creation is the work of the Creator's hands," Peter proclaimed. "It is a gift, a trust, and a reflection of His glory. Let us care for it with diligence and love, for in doing so, we honor Him. Protect the earth, restore its beauty, and live as stewards of His creation, for this is His command and our calling."

Peter's testimony stirred his listeners deeply. Some resolved to change their daily habits, reducing waste and conserving resources. Others felt called to advocate for environmental protection, using their voices to defend the Creator's creation.

Through his words, Peter emphasized the sacred duty of stewardship. Caring for creation was not merely a response to environmental concerns but an act of worship and obedience, a way of living out the Creator's love.

And as Peter continued to proclaim the vision, he prayed that all who heard would embrace their calling as caretakers of the earth, living in harmony with creation and preparing their hearts for the day when the Creator would make all things new.

Chapter 51
The Pursuit of Peace

The vision unfolded in a turbulent scene, where nations waged war, communities were divided by hatred, and individuals bore the weight of conflict in their hearts. Yet, amidst the chaos, Peter saw glimpses of peace—a child offering a hand to another, neighbors reconciling, and fields once burned by war now blooming with life. This was the Creator's call to humanity: to pursue peace in a world fractured by sin.

"Blessed are the peacemakers," the voice declared, filled with both resolve and compassion. "For they shall be called the children of God. My kingdom is one of peace, and my people must walk in my ways."

Peter's gaze turned to the Messiah, the Prince of Peace. He saw Him calming the storm with a word, healing the wounded, and proclaiming a kingdom not of violence but of love. Even as He faced betrayal and death, His response was one of forgiveness and reconciliation.

"This is my peace," the voice said. "It is not as the world gives, fleeting and conditional, but a peace that transcends understanding. My Son gave His life so that peace might reign in hearts, families, and nations."

The vision shifted to humanity's struggle to embrace peace. Peter saw individuals consumed by anger, families torn apart by grudges, and nations justifying war in the name of power and pride. Yet he also witnessed the Spirit moving within hearts, softening them and planting seeds of reconciliation.

"Peace begins within," the voice explained. "A heart at war cannot bring peace to others. Let my Spirit transform you, filling you with my peace, so that you may be a light in the darkness."

Peter was shown the cost of pursuing peace. He saw peacemakers standing in the breach, speaking truth to power, and advocating for reconciliation. Some were scorned, others persecuted, yet their efforts bore fruit—relationships healed, communities restored, and barriers broken down.

"Peacemaking is not passive," the voice said. "It is the work of the courageous, those who are willing to lay down their pride and even their lives for the sake of others. In this, they reflect my heart and my kingdom."

The vision turned to the practical ways the faithful could pursue peace. Peter saw individuals mediating conflicts, offering forgiveness, and creating spaces where dialogue and understanding could flourish. He witnessed communities building bridges between divided groups, fostering unity and mutual respect.

"Peace is not merely the absence of conflict," the voice declared. "It is the presence of justice, compassion, and truth. Let my people work tirelessly for peace, that my kingdom may come on earth as it is in Heaven."

Peter's spirit was drawn to the promise of ultimate peace. He saw the New Jerusalem, where swords were beaten into plowshares and nations no longer learned war. The faithful walked together in harmony, their hearts at rest in the Creator's presence.

"This is my promise," the voice said. "A kingdom of peace, where love reigns and fear is no more. Live now as citizens of this kingdom, bringing its light to a world in need."

The vision revealed the eternal significance of peace. Peter saw how even small acts of peacemaking echoed into eternity, their impact shaping lives and communities for generations. Each effort, though challenging, was a step toward the Creator's ultimate plan of restoration.

"Do not grow weary," the voice declared. "Every act of peace is a reflection of my will and a glimpse of my coming kingdom. Blessed are those who pursue peace, for they walk in my footsteps."

As the vision concluded, Peter was reminded of the urgency of the call to pursue peace. It was not merely an ideal but a command, essential to living in obedience to the Creator and reflecting His love to the world.

"Let my peace rule in your hearts," the voice said. "Be peacemakers, not merely peacekeepers, for the work of reconciliation is my work. In this, you will show the world that you are mine."

When Peter returned from the vision, his heart was filled with both determination and hope. The pursuit of peace was not easy, but it was the path of the faithful, a calling that reflected the Creator's character and kingdom.

He gathered the faithful and spoke of what he had seen, his voice steady yet filled with resolve.

"Peace is the will of the Creator," Peter proclaimed. "It begins in our hearts and flows outward to the world. Let us be peacemakers, bridging divides, healing wounds, and reflecting the love of the Messiah. For in pursuing peace, we walk in His light and prepare the way for His kingdom."

Peter's testimony stirred his listeners deeply. Some resolved to mend broken relationships, while others felt called to work for peace in their communities and beyond.

Through his words, Peter emphasized the transformative power of peace. It was not passive but active, requiring courage, humility, and unwavering faith in the Creator's promises.

And as Peter continued to proclaim the vision, he prayed that all who heard would embrace the call to pursue peace, living as ambassadors of the Creator's kingdom and preparing their hearts for the day when His peace would reign forever.

Chapter 52
The Value of Human Life

The vision opened with a radiant figure holding a delicate thread of light, representing the gift of life itself. Peter stood among countless threads, each one unique yet connected to a larger tapestry. The sight was breathtaking, revealing the sacred nature of every human being, created in the image of the Creator and endowed with purpose and worth.

"This is my creation," the voice declared, filled with tenderness and authority. "Each life is a reflection of my glory, a masterpiece woven by my hand. Let no one diminish what I have made."

Peter's gaze turned to the moment of humanity's creation. He saw the Creator breathing life into Adam, forming him from the dust with care and intention. This act of creation was not impersonal but intimate, a testament to the Creator's love for each individual.

"In my image, I created them," the voice said. "Male and female, they bear my likeness. Every life is sacred, from the moment of its beginning to its fulfillment in eternity."

The vision shifted to the life of the Messiah, where the value of human life was exemplified. Peter saw Him reaching out to the marginalized, healing the sick, and defending the dignity of the oppressed. Each interaction was an affirmation of the inherent worth of every person, regardless of their status or past.

"My Son came to give life," the voice declared. "And life in abundance. Through Him, the value of every soul is revealed, for He gave His life as a ransom for all."

Peter was shown the ways humanity had failed to honor the value of life. He saw wars that claimed countless lives, systems of oppression that dehumanized the vulnerable, and individuals consumed by hatred and violence. Yet he also witnessed acts of courage and compassion—people risking everything to protect and uplift others.

"Sin distorts my creation," the voice said. "It blinds humanity to the worth of their brothers and sisters. Yet my Spirit moves within the faithful, calling them to see as I see, to love as I love."

The vision turned to the responsibility of the faithful in upholding the value of human life. Peter saw believers standing against injustice, advocating for the voiceless, and providing care for the sick, the poor, and the vulnerable. These acts of service were not mere charity but a reflection of the Creator's heart.

"To love your neighbor is to honor their worth," the voice declared. "And to love your enemies is to affirm their place in my creation. Let my people be a light, showing the world the sacredness of life through their words and actions."

Peter's spirit was drawn to the connection between the value of human life and the Creator's eternal plan. He saw the faithful gathered in the New Jerusalem, each life contributing to the beauty of the whole. The scars of injustice were healed, and every soul was restored to its intended glory.

"This is my kingdom," the voice said. "A place where every life is honored, every tear is wiped away, and every heart is made whole. Let my people live now as citizens of this kingdom, reflecting its values in the present."

The vision revealed practical ways the faithful could affirm the value of human life. Peter saw acts of kindness, such as feeding the hungry, comforting the grieving, and advocating for the oppressed. He also saw efforts to protect life at all stages, from the unborn to the elderly, ensuring that no one was forgotten or dismissed.

"Do not grow weary in doing good," the voice said. "For each act of love, no matter how small, is a proclamation of my truth. Through you, the world will see the worth of every life."

As the vision concluded, Peter was reminded of the Creator's unwavering love for humanity. The value of human life was not based on accomplishments or status but on the simple truth that each person was made in the Creator's image and cherished by Him.

"Love one another as I have loved you," the voice declared. "In this, you honor me and reflect my glory. Let every word, every action, affirm the worth of those I have made."

When Peter returned from the vision, his heart was filled with both conviction and compassion. The value of human life was not merely an ideal but a truth that demanded action, a reflection of the Creator's own nature.

He gathered the faithful and spoke of what he had seen, his voice steady yet filled with passion.

"Every life is sacred," Peter proclaimed. "From the least to the greatest, each person bears the image of the Creator. Let us honor one another, defend the vulnerable, and proclaim the worth of every soul. In doing so, we fulfill His command and prepare our hearts for His kingdom."

Peter's testimony stirred his listeners deeply. Some resolved to advocate for the oppressed and the voiceless, while others felt called to serve in their communities, ensuring that every person was treated with dignity and respect.

Through his words, Peter emphasized the transformative power of affirming the value of human life. It was not only a reflection of faith but a call to action, a way of living out the Creator's love in a world that often failed to see its worth.

And as Peter continued to proclaim the vision, he prayed that all who heard would embrace the sacredness of life, living as witnesses to the Creator's love and preparing their hearts for the day when His kingdom would be fully realized.

Chapter 53
Individual Responsibility

The vision unfolded in a bustling city, where countless lives intertwined, each person engaged in their unique tasks and pursuits. Peter observed the intricate web of relationships and actions, how one choice rippled outward, affecting countless others. Yet, within the complexity of the scene, the importance of each individual's responsibility stood out—a call to live with intention, faith, and accountability.

"This is my design," the voice declared, filled with clarity and purpose. "Each life is a thread in the fabric of my creation. Your choices matter, your actions have weight, and your responsibility is both personal and profound."

Peter's gaze turned to the Creator's gift of free will, a reflection of His love and trust. He saw humanity empowered to choose between good and evil, light and darkness. This freedom, though often misused, was central to humanity's purpose: to love the Creator and serve others with intentionality and care.

"I have set before you life and death," the voice said. "Choose life, that you may live. Each choice you make shapes not only your path but the world around you."

The vision shifted to the life of the Messiah, the perfect example of individual responsibility. Peter saw Him serving others tirelessly, teaching truth, and fulfilling His mission with unwavering resolve. Even in moments of great suffering, the Messiah took responsibility for the salvation of humanity, demonstrating the power of obedience and sacrifice.

"My Son lived as a servant," the voice declared. "He bore the burdens of others, yet He was never without purpose. His life was a testimony to the power of faithfulness, and through Him, the path to life was revealed."

Peter was shown how individual responsibility extended to the care of others. He saw individuals feeding the hungry, comforting the lonely, and standing against injustice. These acts, though often small, created ripples of change, transforming lives and communities.

"Your responsibility is not only to yourself," the voice explained. "It is to your neighbor, to the stranger, and to the least among you. As you serve others, you serve me."

The vision turned to the dangers of neglecting individual responsibility. Peter saw people consumed by selfishness, their choices leading to harm and division. Yet he also saw the Creator's mercy calling them back, offering grace and a chance to begin anew.

"Do not grow weary in doing good," the voice said. "For though you may stumble, my grace is sufficient. Take up your responsibility with courage, for I am with you always."

Peter's spirit was drawn to the interconnectedness of individual actions. He saw how seemingly small decisions—an act of kindness, a moment of honesty, a step toward forgiveness—could lead to profound impacts. Each person's responsibility, when embraced, contributed to the Creator's greater plan.

"Faithfulness in little things leads to greater things," the voice declared. "Your actions, no matter how small, are not forgotten. I see them, and I honor them."

The vision revealed the eternal significance of individual responsibility. Peter saw the faithful standing before the Creator, their lives a testimony to their choices. Each act of obedience, each moment of faith, had been woven into the tapestry of the Creator's kingdom, bringing glory to His name.

"Well done, good and faithful servant," the voice said. "You have been faithful over little; I will set you over much. Enter into the joy of your Lord."

As the vision concluded, Peter was reminded of the weight and joy of individual responsibility. It was not a burden to be feared but a privilege to be embraced, a way to reflect the Creator's love and contribute to His kingdom.

"Walk in my ways," the voice said. "Take responsibility for your choices, your actions, and your faith. In this, you honor me and fulfill the purpose for which you were created."

When Peter returned from the vision, his heart was filled with resolve and hope. Individual responsibility was not a solitary endeavor but a partnership with the Creator, a daily act of faith and obedience.

He gathered the faithful and spoke of what he had seen, his voice steady yet filled with encouragement.

"Each of us has been given a purpose," Peter proclaimed. "Our choices matter, our actions have power, and our lives are a testimony to the Creator's grace. Let us take responsibility for what we have been entrusted with, serving Him and one another with faithfulness and love."

Peter's testimony stirred his listeners deeply. Some resolved to take greater responsibility in their families and communities, while others felt called to pursue acts of service and faithfulness they had long delayed.

Through his words, Peter emphasized the transformative power of individual responsibility. It was not about perfection but about faithfulness, a daily commitment to live in alignment with the Creator's will.

And as Peter continued to proclaim the vision, he prayed that all who heard would embrace their calling, living with purpose and integrity as they prepared their hearts for the eternal joy of the Creator's kingdom.

Chapter 54
The Legacy of the Apocalypse of Peter

The vision began with a scroll, glowing faintly in the dim light of a vast hall. Around it stood countless figures, each representing an age, a culture, or a community. The Apocalypse of Peter, with its profound revelations and stirring imagery, had left a lasting mark on humanity. Its legacy extended far beyond the text itself, influencing thought, art, and faith across the centuries.

"This is my word," the voice declared, steady and solemn. "It is not bound by time, for its truths are eternal. The visions given to Peter speak to all who seek understanding, hope, and the promise of my justice and mercy."

Peter's gaze turned to the early church, where the Apocalypse had first been shared. He saw communities gathering in homes, reading the words of his vision with reverence. They found comfort in its promises, strength in its warnings, and encouragement in its descriptions of the eternal kingdom.

"These words were given to prepare and to inspire," the voice said. "They reminded my people of what is to come, urging them to live in readiness and faith. Through them, the church was strengthened in times of trial."

The vision shifted to the halls of academia and art, where the Apocalypse of Peter had inspired theologians, poets, and painters. Peter saw vivid frescoes of paradise and judgment, sermons that called for repentance, and writings that explored the mysteries of divine justice. These works carried the vision into new generations, keeping its message alive.

"My revelation is not for one moment alone," the voice declared. "It speaks to all who have ears to hear. Through the creativity of my people, its truths are revealed anew, drawing others to my light."

Peter was shown how the Apocalypse of Peter shaped debates about salvation, justice, and eternity. He saw councils deliberating over its place in scripture, scholars grappling with its warnings, and preachers interpreting its meaning for their congregations. These discussions, though sometimes divisive, deepened humanity's understanding of the Creator's will.

"Truth invites reflection," the voice said. "It challenges, it provokes, and it refines. The words I gave to Peter are not meant to be idle—they are a call to action, a summons to consider your place in my eternal plan."

The vision turned to the hearts of individuals who had been touched by the Apocalypse. Peter saw a young woman moved to repentance after reading its descriptions of judgment, a grieving father comforted by its promises of paradise, and a weary worker finding hope in its assurance of justice.

"My word does not return void," the voice declared. "It accomplishes what I intend, reaching the hearts of those who are ready to hear. Through Peter's vision, lives have been changed, and souls drawn closer to me."

Peter's spirit was drawn to the responsibility of preserving and sharing the Apocalypse's message. He saw scribes copying its words with care, translators bringing it to new languages, and teachers explaining its truths to those eager to learn. This legacy, though carried by human hands, was sustained by the Creator's Spirit.

"My truth endures," the voice said. "Though human hands may falter, my Spirit guides and protects. Let my people be faithful stewards of this revelation, ensuring that its light is not hidden."

The vision revealed the ongoing relevance of the Apocalypse of Peter. Peter saw future generations facing trials and uncertainties, yet finding solace in its words. The vision's themes of justice, mercy, and hope resonated across time, a timeless message for a changing world.

"This is my promise," the voice declared. "What I have revealed to Peter is not merely for his time but for all time. Its legacy is eternal, for it speaks of the eternal."

As the vision concluded, Peter was reminded of the sacredness of his calling. The Apocalypse he had received was not his alone—it belonged to all who sought the Creator and longed for His kingdom. Its legacy was not static but dynamic, continuing to shape lives and communities in profound ways.

"Guard what I have entrusted to you," the voice said. "Share it with boldness and humility, that its light may shine in the darkness. Through you, my word will endure, and my people will be prepared for the day of my coming."

When Peter returned from the vision, his heart was filled with awe and gratitude. The legacy of the Apocalypse of Peter was not merely in its words but in its impact—a living testimony to the Creator's truth and love.

He gathered the faithful and spoke of what he had seen, his voice steady yet filled with reverence.

"The vision I received is a gift for all generations," Peter proclaimed. "It calls us to repentance, offers us hope, and prepares us for eternity. Let us honor its legacy by living its truths, sharing its message, and trusting in the promises it reveals. For its words are not mine but the Creator's, and they endure forever."

Peter's testimony stirred his listeners deeply. Some felt renewed urgency to study the Apocalypse, while others resolved to share its message with those who had yet to hear.

Through his words, Peter emphasized the enduring power of the vision. It was not a relic of the past but a living revelation, calling all who heard to respond in faith and obedience.

And as Peter continued to proclaim the vision, he prayed that all who heard would honor its legacy, living as witnesses to its truth and preparing their hearts for the day when its promises would be fully realized in the Creator's eternal kingdom.

Chapter 55
Humanity's Future

The vision unfolded with a vast panorama of the earth, spinning slowly in the Creator's hands. Peter stood at the edge of this unfolding story, witnessing the possibilities that lay before humanity. The future was a tapestry yet to be fully woven, its threads shaped by the choices of individuals, the faith of communities, and the sovereign will of the Creator.

"This is what lies ahead," the voice declared, resonant with both hope and warning. "Humanity's future is in my hands, yet I have given you the power to choose the path you will walk. Will you follow me into life, or turn away into darkness?"

Peter's gaze turned to humanity's potential for good. He saw acts of love and kindness ripple outward, transforming lives and communities. He witnessed advancements in knowledge and technology used to heal the sick, feed the hungry, and restore the earth. These glimpses of the future were radiant with the Creator's light, a reflection of His kingdom breaking into the present.

"This is what I desire," the voice said. "That humanity walks in my ways, reflecting my image through their love for one another and their stewardship of my creation. In this, my glory is revealed."

The vision shifted to the consequences of sin and rebellion. Peter saw wars ravaging the earth, greed consuming its resources, and humanity turning away from the Creator's call. The future became dark, marked by suffering and separation, the result of choices made without regard for the Creator's will.

"Sin leads to destruction," the voice declared. "When humanity rejects my ways, they sow chaos and reap despair. Yet even in the darkness, my light shines, and my call remains: repent, and turn back to me."

Peter was shown the role of the faithful in shaping humanity's future. He saw believers standing as beacons of hope, their lives a testimony to the Creator's love and truth. Through their actions, they brought healing to broken systems, reconciliation to divided communities, and the Gospel to those who had not yet heard.

"You are the light of the world," the voice said. "Through you, I work to bring my kingdom to earth. Be faithful in the small things, and you will see my power revealed in the great."

The vision turned to the ultimate culmination of humanity's story. Peter saw the day when the Creator would make all things new, restoring the earth and gathering His people into the eternal kingdom. This future was not merely an ideal but a promise, a certainty rooted in the Creator's faithfulness.

"My plans cannot be thwarted," the voice declared. "Though the world may falter, my purpose stands firm. I will bring justice to the nations, peace to the earth, and joy to my people. Trust in me, for the future is mine."

Peter's spirit was drawn to the tension between hope and responsibility. The future was secure in the Creator's hands, yet humanity's role in shaping the present remained vital. Every act of love, every step of faith, contributed to the unfolding of the Creator's plan.

"Work while it is day," the voice said. "For the night is coming when no one can work. Let my people live with urgency and purpose, knowing that their labor is not in vain."

The vision revealed practical ways humanity could embrace the Creator's call for the future. Peter saw families teaching their children to love and serve, communities caring for the vulnerable, and nations seeking justice and peace. These efforts, though imperfect, were steps toward the eternal kingdom.

"Do not despise the small beginnings," the voice declared. "For each act of faithfulness builds upon another, drawing the world closer to my design. In your hands, I have placed the seeds of the future—tend them with care."

As the vision concluded, Peter was reminded of the hope that anchored humanity's future. It was not found in human strength or wisdom but in the Creator's promises, fulfilled through the Messiah and sustained by His Spirit.

"My plans for you are good," the voice said. "Plans to prosper you and not to harm you, plans to give you hope and a future. Walk in my ways, and you will see the fulfillment of all I have promised."

When Peter returned from the vision, his heart was filled with both urgency and peace. Humanity's future was not predetermined by its failures but shaped by its response to the Creator's call.

He gathered the faithful and spoke of what he had seen, his voice steady yet filled with hope.

"The future is in the hands of the Creator," Peter proclaimed. "Yet we are called to be His co-workers, shaping the present with faith, love, and obedience. Let us walk in His light, trusting in His promises, and working for His kingdom, knowing that the best is yet to come."

Peter's testimony stirred his listeners deeply. Some resolved to take action in their communities, bringing hope to the broken and faith to the lost. Others found renewed strength to face their own challenges, trusting in the Creator's plans for their lives.

Through his words, Peter emphasized the balance between divine sovereignty and human responsibility. Humanity's future was secure in the Creator's hands, yet each person's choices mattered, contributing to the unfolding of His kingdom.

And as Peter continued to proclaim the vision, he prayed that all who heard would embrace the hope of the future, living with purpose and faith as they prepared their hearts for the eternal joy of the Creator's kingdom.

Epilogue

The vision unfolded in radiant glory, revealing the culmination of all that Peter had seen and proclaimed. He stood at the edge of eternity, gazing upon the New Jerusalem, where the Creator dwelled with His people. The light of His presence filled every corner, and the voices of the faithful rose in a song that echoed through the heavens. This was the fulfillment of every promise, the answer to every longing, the eternal hope realized.

"This is my dwelling place," the voice declared, filled with love and majesty. "I have made all things new. My people are with me, and I am their God. The journey is complete, yet my joy with them will never end."

Peter's gaze turned to the gates of the city, open wide to all who had walked in faith. He saw the nations streaming in, their diversity a testament to the Creator's vast and unending love. Every tribe, tongue, and people were represented, united in the eternal kingdom.

"My grace has gathered them," the voice said. "Not by their merit, but by my love. They have washed their robes in the blood of the Lamb and now walk in my light forever."

The vision shifted to the tree of life, its leaves bringing healing to the nations. Peter saw how every wound, every sorrow, every division had been mended. The faithful, who had endured trials and suffering, now stood whole and radiant, their tears wiped away by the Creator's hand.

"There is no more pain here," the voice declared. "No mourning, no death, no darkness. My light shines, and my people live in joy unending."

Peter was shown the river of life, flowing from the throne of the Creator and the Lamb. Its waters were clear as crystal, bringing renewal to all who drank. The faithful gathered around its banks, their hearts overflowing with gratitude and worship.

"This is the life I promised," the voice said. "It is abundant, eternal, and unshaken. Those who thirsted have been satisfied, and those who hungered have been filled. This is their inheritance, prepared since the foundation of the world."

The vision turned to the Lamb, standing at the center of the city. Peter saw the marks of His sacrifice, now transformed into a symbol of victory and love. The Lamb's presence was the light of the kingdom, illuminating every heart and every corner of eternity.

"My Son is the Alpha and the Omega," the voice declared. "Through Him, all things have been made new. His sacrifice has reconciled creation to me, and His reign is forever."

Peter's spirit was drawn to the faithful who had heard the message of the Apocalypse. He saw how they had lived in hope, sharing the Gospel, caring for others, and walking in obedience. Their lives, though imperfect, had been a testimony to the Creator's love and faithfulness.

"They are my witnesses," the voice said. "They held fast to my promises, even in the face of trial. Now they rest in my presence, their joy complete and their work fulfilled."

The vision revealed the eternal song of the redeemed, a melody of praise that filled the heavens. Peter saw how every act of faith, every step of obedience, and every word of love had contributed to this song. The faithful, from every generation, joined together in perfect harmony, their voices declaring the Creator's glory.

"This is the song of eternity," the voice declared. "It is the song of redemption, the song of love, the song of life. It will never end, for my people are with me, and I am with them."

As the vision concluded, Peter was filled with a sense of peace and completion. The Apocalypse was not merely a revelation of judgment but a promise of restoration, a call to hope, and an invitation to eternal joy.

"The end is the beginning," the voice said. "Go and proclaim what you have seen, for my words are faithful and true. Let all who hear come to me, that they may share in the life I have prepared."

When Peter returned from the vision, his heart was filled with awe and gratitude. The journey of the Apocalypse had revealed the Creator's justice, mercy, and love, calling all who heard to respond in faith and obedience.

He gathered the faithful one final time and spoke of what he had seen, his voice steady yet filled with reverence.

"The vision is complete," Peter proclaimed. "The Creator has shown us His plan—to bring justice, to offer mercy, and to dwell with us forever. Let us live as those who believe, sharing His love, walking in His light, and preparing our hearts for His eternal kingdom. For the Lamb has triumphed, and His reign is forever."

Peter's final testimony stirred his listeners deeply. Some wept with joy, others knelt in worship, and all resolved to live in light of the promises they had heard.

Through his words, Peter left a legacy of hope, faith, and love. The Apocalypse was not an end but a beginning, a call to live with purpose and prepare for the eternal joy of the Creator's presence.

And as Peter's voice faded, the faithful carried the vision forward, proclaiming its message to the world, until the day when every knee would bow, every tongue confess, and all creation join in the eternal song of the Lamb.

www.ingramcontent.com/pod-product-compliance
Lightning Source LLC
LaVergne TN
LVHW040055080526
838202LV00045B/3645